The Banalization of Nihilism

The Banalization of Nihilism

Twentieth-Century Responses to Meaninglessness

Karen L. Carr

STATE UNIVERSITY OF NEW YORK PRESS

Published by
State University of New York Press, Albany

Printed in the United States of America

For information, address State University of New York
Press, State University Plaza, Albany, N.Y. 12246

Production by Marilyn P. Semerad
Marketing by Bernadette LaManna

Library of Congress Cataloging-in-Publication Data

Carr, Karen Leslie.
The banalization of nihilism : twentieth-century responses to meaninglessness / Karen L. Carr.
p. cm.
Rev. of the author's thesis (Ph. D.—Stanford University, 1989) presented under title: The birth, baptism, and banalization of nihilism.
Includes bibliographical references and index.
ISBN 0-7914-0833-7 (hardcover). — ISBN 0-7914-0834-5 (paperback)
1. Meaninglessness (Philosophy) 2. Nihilism (Philosophy)
3. Philosophy, Modern—20th century. I. Title.
B825.2.C37 1992
149'.8—dc20

90-27104
CIP

10 9 8 7 6 5 4 3 2 1

To my bugs

Contents

Acknowledgments

Many people have read and commented on various versions of this work, from its inception at Stanford University through its completion at Lawrence University; to all I am indebted. I owe a special debt, however, to Van A. Harvey, who helped me tame an unruly subject and who provided a model of scholarship I have striven to emulate, here and elsewhere. Thanks are also due Michelle M. Mattson, for her guidance on a number of the translations, and Kristin A. Baum, for her work readying the text for publication. Finally, without Peter Glick's patient counsel and encouragement, the work would never have reached its present form.

I am grateful to Oxford University Press for permission to quote from Karl Barth's *Epistle to the Romans*. Portions of Chapter Three have appeared as "Nietzsche on Nihilism and the Crisis of Interpretation" in *Soundings* 73:1 (1990), 85–106. Several grants provided by Lawrence University helped ensure the continuation of this project.

Acknowledgments

Part I

The Uncanniest of All Guests

1

The Problem of Nihilism

One of the most striking features of post–World-War-I religious thought is its exploitation of the experience of meaninglessness as the basis for Christian apologetics. In a well-known commentary on Paul's "Letter to the Romans,"[1] Karl Barth described faith in a way intended to shatter all prior conceptions of the religious life. Faith, according to Barth, is a void (*ein Hohlraum*), a "not knowing" that is characterized by the absence of belief, conviction, and confidence rather than by their presence. An individual is genuinely religious, Barth seemed to suggest, when he or she is most forlorn, despairing of every possibility of truth, estranged from all value and meaning, lost in "a condition of shattering confusion, from which he can never escape" (*Romans*, 85). The experience of the impotence of knowledge and the futility of action—of the senseless, empty quality of life—was portrayed as the condition, indeed the only condition, of religious affirmation.

Had this work fallen stillborn from the press, it would today be little more than an intellectual curiosity, interesting, perhaps, for its peculiar juxtaposition of faith and what appears to be a form of nihilism, but not something warranting sustained attention. But the impassioned rhetoric of the then-unknown pastor from Safenwil was hardly stillborn; in the words of one contemporary, it "fell like a bomb on the playground of the theologians."[2] Not only did it serve as the avowed manifesto of Dialectical Theology, or the Theology of Crisis[3] (whose members included Emil Brunner, Friedrich Gogarten, and Eduard Thurneysen, as well as Barth himself), but more than any other single work of Protestant thought, its appearance marked the break with the liberal theological tradition that had flourished for nearly a century. Even those thinkers who found Barth's views problematic or repellent were forced to take his position seriously; consequently the importance of this work for understanding twentieth-century religious thought in the West is unsurpassed.

Barth's *Roemerbrief* becomes all the more important when one realizes that the emphasis on meaninglessness as the ground of the genuinely human life was not limited to the theological sphere. Most of the thinkers loosely grouped together under the title "existentialist"[4] similarly stressed that the loss of meaning and confidence in one's life is the basis—or at least the beginning—of what they termed authentic existence. Although the precise terminology varied, the work of Heidegger and Jaspers in Germany, and of Sartre and Camus in France, shared this preoccupation with meaninglessness and the conviction that its confrontation is instrumental in the positive affirmation of life.

While the ways in which this preoccupation was expressed were diverse, *Der Roemerbrief* throws into relief the underlying logic shared by most of the existential thinkers in the first half of the twentieth century. The goal was to wrest positive benefit from a condition which seemed paralyzing and inescapable: the advent of nihilism, the loss of all sense of contact with anything that is ultimately true or meaningful. The collapse of the liberal paradigm on the battlefields of the First World War, the corresponding loss of confidence in reason and history, and a growing sense of the sterility of romantic subjectivity created a great emptiness that both needed to be filled and yet seemed impossible to satisfy. The dialectical theologians' attempt to make this condition a prerequisite for genuine religious faith was but an extreme instance of a more widespread trend to transform an apparently unavoidable state into a virtue. Thus when Friedrich Gogarten wrote in 1920 that "the last and deepest source reveals itself only at that point at which all our foundations have been destroyed, have become worthless and meaningless" and that "only in this state of meaninglessness can the eternal meaning of all things shine through,"[5] he was expressing essentially the same sentiment one finds in Heidegger's early claims about the revelatory power of anxiety or in Camus' portrait of the existential hero as the individual who lives in self-conscious confrontation with a meaningless world, refusing either to deny or succumb to its power.[6]

What unites these somewhat disparate thinkers is their desire to embrace a condition that many of their peers found disastrous and cataclysmic. As the twentieth century unfolded, it became increasingly difficult to deny that the combined legacy of the eighteenth and nineteenth centuries was dubious at best, for it had left its heirs with, on the one hand, a conviction of the desirability, even the necessity of truth and, on the other hand, a radical suspicion of all claims to have found truth. The existentialist response—to focus on precisely this absence of any legitimate ground, outside the commitment of the individual, upon which to stand—was widely criticized as pessimistic, even nihilistic. This criticism stemmed not so much from the fact that the existentialists pointed to a world of purely human origin and found its promise of meaning counterfeit, but because they seemed to welcome this void, even to cultivate it, as a necessary aspect of human existence.

In many ways, the existentialists and the dialectical theologians were pursuing a path first cleared by Nietzsche more than fifty years earlier. While the term "nihilism" had been in use throughout the nineteenth century (and perhaps even earlier)[7] Nietzsche was the first thinker to recognize both the severity of its implications and the subtlety of its origins. His published works, deconstructing with polemical glee both Judeo-Christian morality and the metaphysical pretensions of the philosophical tradition in which it was embedded, are but the tip of an iceberg made up of hundreds of notebook entries exploring the significance and the consequences of the advent of nihilism. Dubbing it "the uncanniest of all guests," Nietzsche believed nihilism to be "one of the greatest crises, a moment of the deepest self-reflection, of humanity."[8] Characterizing it as a disease that was pathological in its intensity, Nietzsche nonetheless thought that nihilism had within it the possibility of redemption from an interpretation of life that was both hypocritical and debilitating. If the positive content of Nietzsche's vision of the individual redeemed through and by nihilism is unclear, his conviction that such redemption was in fact a concrete possibility is not. And while one might argue with many of the specifics of Barth's view of the "new man" and Rudolf Bultmann's portrayal of the authenticity of life of faith, these attempts to make nihilism a source of affirmation were fulfilling the spirit, if not the letter, of Nietzsche's thought.[9]

The irony that Nietzsche, despite his contempt for theologians and all that was theological,[10] nonetheless served as inspiration for one of the most significant movements in twentieth-century theology makes an inquiry into the religious appropriation of nihilism a fascinating study. There is something both provocative and perverse in the often grim insistence of the dialectical theologians that the dissolution of sense is the beginning of real meaning. Central to their construction of what could be called a "soteriology of ambiguity" were two related beliefs: an understanding of nihilism as the loss of something deemed desirable, even necessary, for human survival, coupled with a conviction of the importance and value of truthfulness in the face of such a loss.

Both of these attitudes can be traced to Nietzsche, and both were necessary for the dialectical theologians' position to be intelligible. It was precisely the tension between what one wanted—in this case, a transcendental meaning or ground accessible to human inquiry—and the realization that this could never be had which provided the content for the vision of humanity they espoused. The despair bred of this tension was constitutive of human existence, they argued; recognizing and accepting the basic ambiguity of all human endeavors despite one's ineradicable need for certainty was made the basis of authenticity among existential thinkers more generally. To be fully human meant to affirm both the utter emptiness of a world devoid of meaning and the human need for a meaningful world. To give up either—to lose oneself in an "ism" purporting to be absolute truth or to deny the fundamental drive for meaning shared by all members of the human race—was, from this point of view, to succumb either to inauthenticity, in the former case, or unthinking animality, in the latter.

The heyday of both dialectical theology and existentialism more generally has passed, not without some justification, for their understanding of the nature of human existence all too easily becomes a hackneyed caricature of itself. More than that, however, there is a sense in which the *angst*-ridden reflections from the first half of this century sound dated, almost comical in their intensity and self-seriousness. One might infer from this that the dangers of nihilism, so vividly painted by Nietzsche, have passed, that the crisis has been resolved, that human reason has resumed its progressive investigation into the true and the good. Yet what in fact has happened in the last two decades is a recasting of the problem of nihilism into a framework so different from that shared by Nietzsche and his unwitting successors that the work of these earlier thinkers is in danger of becoming unintelligible.[11]

This new framework, and the corresponding attitude towards nihilism characteristic of it, is best seen in the works of those thinkers labelled "anti-foundationalists" and "deconstructionists." Bearing many superficial similarities to the thought of the dialectical theologians—and, arguably, that of Nietzsche—the writings of Jacques Derrida in France and Richard Rorty in this country seek to uncover and condemn the absolutist pretensions of, in their eyes, the entire metaphysical tradition of the West. Barth attacked the portrayal of God as an object within the world, accessible to human manipulation and control; Derrida and Rorty criticize the metaphysics of presence and the portrayal of truth as something existing "out there" to be discovered. Barth argued that the investigation of human attempts to conceptualize deity revealed only relativity, ambiguity, and the utter absence of what was pretended to be spoken of; Derrida's famous dictum that "Il n'y a pas de hors-texte" and Rorty's claim that truth is never anything more than the expression of a particular community's values similarly reject the possibility of any transcendental, trans-cultural, or trans-historical access to truth or meaning.[12] Barth claimed to speak from a "point of view that is no point of view" (*Romans,* 58); Derrida similarly tries to speak from a "non-philosophical place," while Rorty repeatedly denies that he is presenting a theory or a philosophical position at all.[13] Thus the religious appropriation of nihilism as a means of announcing the end of theological liberalism prefigured the deconstructive and anti-foundationalist engagement with the same phenomenon to signify the end more generally of the metaphysical tradition of the West.

Despite these striking parallels, there is a fundamental and, in the final analysis, irreconciliable difference between the anti-foundationalism of a Rorty and the dialectical theology of a Barth. While both Rorty and Barth desire to embrace nihilism in some sense, and welcome its presence in human life and discourse, the attitude taken towards this phenomenon differs considerably. Put metaphorically, Barth saw nihilism as a disease signifying the wretchedness of the human condition, whose value lay in forcing us to become aware of precisely this wretchedness; Rorty sees it rather as a cure, which needs no further treatment. Both seek to make nihilism the basis of affirmation, but for Barth this involved a major transformation of the self, whereas for Rorty, and perhaps for Derrida as well, no such transformation is necessary.[14] For Barth, as for existentialism more generally, the advent of nihilism is an occasion for despair; for Rorty, Derrida, and their peers, it is an occasion for at least mild revelry.

The present work explores three "moments" in the history of contemporary nihilism: first, Nietzsche's portrayal of nihilism as a cultural phenomenon linked to a particular historical event—the self-dissolution of Christianity; second, the religious appropriation of nihilism by the dialectical theologians in their attempt to connect it to Christian faith; third, nihilism's domestication in the deconstructive analyses of the anti-foundationalists, typified by Richard Rorty.

My aim is twofold. First, I will show how the appraisal of nihilism has shifted in the last century (in at least some circles) away from something which we must escape to something which is a relatively innocuous characterization of the radically interpretive character of human life. For many postmodernists, the presence of nihilism evokes, not terror, but a yawn. Second, I will discuss the possible origin and implications of this transformation, a transformation which, in my opinion, is not a happy one. To anticipate, I believe that the change evident in these three interpretations and accounts of nihilism is due in part to the recasting of nihilism, understood initially as a historical event, into a phenomenon coextensive with human historicity. Regarded by Nietzsche as a condition created by a particular set of intellectual developments, by the late twentieth century nihilism is seen as implicit in the fact that human beings are historical creatures that must interpret their surroundings. As a result, nihilism ceases to be something from which we must escape, loses its potentially transformative and redemptive power, and becomes instead simply a rather banal characterization of the human situation.

As I shall argue, what we lose when we make this move is far greater than what we gain. While the good news appears to be that we no longer need to worry about a situation that we seem unable to avoid, the bad news is that this transformation essentially reifies the present values, beliefs, and judgments of the historical community to which we belong into absolute truths, albeit unintentionally and unconsciously. At its extreme, banalizing nihilism—which I argue takes place in certain postmodern thinkers, here represented by Rorty—paradoxically results in an absolutism at once pernicious and covert.

The linking of Nietzsche, Barth, and Rorty in making these points might strike some readers as odd; certainly it requires at least brief justification. While the joining of Nietzsche and Rorty seems plausible enough, and the conjunction of Nietzsche and Barth almost, if not equally, plausible, to put the three together might well appear perverse. What was the principle of selection underwriting this choice? What, in other words, justifies the joining of Rorty and the early Karl Barth?[15]

As I read the intellectual history of the twentieth century, Rorty and the early Barth represent opposite poles of interpretation leading away from the liberal heritage of the nineteenth century. Barth typifies what I will call below the "religious" response, Rorty typifies the "aesthetic."[16] While obviously their historical and intellectual peers were different, both speak from and to communities that regard our relationship to the truth as problematic. Both are sensitive to the radically historical nature of human beings and the perspectival, relative nature of human knowledge. Both stand, in other words, in Nietzsche's shadow. The very oddness of their conjunction, in light of this fact, helps make my point—they have pursued two divergent paths in a roughly analogous intellectual milieu. As I will show below, Barth elected to abandon the possibility of knowledge so that he might cling fast to truth, while Rorty turns away from truth in order to save knowledge.[17]

The second chapter briefly outlines the conceptual history of nihilism and distinguishes between various possible uses of the term. This is important because the term "nihilism," while widely used in the last two centuries, has no universally agreed-upon definition; although family resemblances between usages naturally exist, there is enough variation to promote substantial confusion. After viewing some of the more prominent definitions of "nihilism," Chapter Two identifies the sense in which "nihilism" is employed in this work.

The third chapter lays out Nietzsche's interpretation of nihilism and his analysis of its relation to Christianity. Central to Nietzsche's portrayal of nihilism was his conviction that it was a major crisis in the history of European culture, a turning point that would signify either the beginning of our demise or the starting point of a new way of being in the world. The ambiguity Nietzsche attributed to nihilism was of fundamental importance for subsequent attempts to wrest redemptive force from this crisis. Nietzsche offered the first sustained analysis of nihilism as a cultural malaise, thereby giving birth to the understanding of nihilism that informed the first half of the twentieth century.

Chapter Four explores the religious response to the advent of nihilism in the work of the dialectical theologians by examining their most formative work, Karl Barth's *Roemerbrief.* Here the historical context of the emergence of nihilism is in effect denied, nihilism being transformed into God's judgment upon humanity. The confrontation with nihilism throws the individual back upon him- or herself, raising the question, "Who, then, am I?" This existential self-questioning is made the basis of faith, or authenticity, as Bultmann's interpretation of Barth illustrates. Fundamental to this turn is the preservation of the crisis-value attributed to nihilism by Nietzsche, for only in the jolt of having one's illusions shattered does nihilism serve as a revelation of something beyond itself. The dialectical theologians baptized nihilism, in effect, by linking it both to the sinfulness of the human condition—the recognition of which is necessary for genuine religious faith—and the gracious love of

God. The experience of annihilation becomes "God's way of saving us."

The fifth chapter examines Rorty's anti-foundationalist reading of Western philosophy and his deconstruction of the philosophical and ethical search for truth and goodness as a form of bad faith. Rorty domesticates nihilism by making it an unobjectionable characteristic of human thought and discourse. Nihilism has been completely divested of its power to shock, and therefore of its power to reveal and redeem. We are left only with the prescriptions of a community, a community which it seems impossible to change without falling prey to a form of bad consciousness.

Thus the goal of this work is to show how Nietzsche's "uncanniest of all guests," the bane of the nineteenth century, is becoming an unremarkable, even banal, feature of modern life. The concluding chapter presents my analysis of how this transformation has happened and explores some of its implications. Nihilism, I will argue, comes full circle—as its crisis value diminishes, as it becomes accepted with an indifferent shrug, it devolves into its antithesis: a dogmatic absolutism.

While the presence of nihilism in our midst is widely acknowledged, there have been few attempts to trace its history or to document changes in our interpretation of it. Those works which do exist are generally marked either by a polemicism which may make them interesting reading, but renders their scholarly value problematic, or by a narrowness of focus which limits their usefulness.[18] Without exception nihilism is portrayed as a monolithic phenomenon which has not changed since its discovery. The present work is an attempt to offer a larger picture of the history of nihilism, showing both that the appraisal of nihilism has changed over the last century, and how it has changed. Thus it seeks to begin to fill an important gap in scholarly reflections on the modern period. The fact that the word "nihilism" was coined within the last two centuries suggests that nihilism and modernity are somehow coextensive phenomena. If indeed this is the case, then only when we understand something about the range and breadth of contemporary interpretations of nihilism are we in a position to begin to understand and evaluate the cultural climate in which we find ourselves.

2

Understanding Nihilism

The root of the word "nihilism" is the Latin *nihil,* literally meaning "not anything, nothing; that which does not exist" (*Oxford Latin Dictionary*). The same root appears in the verb "annihilate," meaning, "to reduce to non-existence, to blot out of existence."[1] While many commentators on nihilism agree with Stanley Rosen's view that it is "a perennial human possibility,"[2] the term was not actually coined until the late eighteenth century—coextensive, in other words, with the emergence of the Enlightenment.

There is some dispute about where the term first originated; some credit its creation to J. H. Obereit (1787), while others point to F. Jenisch (1796) or Friedrich Schlegel (1797).[3] All agree, however, that the word first received sustained philosophical attention in the first decade of the nineteenth century in the debates about the implications of German idealism.[4] It was Jacobi who either borrowed or coined the term to characterize what he regarded as the unpleasant consequences of the regnant philosophical school, transcendental idealism, in his *Sendschriften an Fichte.*[5] In this short piece, Jacobi criticized the implicit tendency of transcendental idealism to dissolve the reality of the external world into the "nothingness" of consciousness by focusing on the subjective conditions for the possibility of knowledge. Idealism culminates, according to Jacobi, in mere "chimerism, or nihilism (*nihilismus*)"; to his mind, this objection demonstrated the untenability of idealism. Clearly for Jacobi, "nihilism" was a term of reproach, a slur of sufficient proportions that it almost functioned as an argument *reductio ad absurdum*. If one could show that nihilism was the consequence of a particular position, then that position was obviously invalid.

Jacobi was not alone in regarding nihilism as an undesirable position; most of his contemporaries also regarded it as a philosophical indictment of the highest order.[6] Hegel was a partial, if curious, exception to this general truth. Although he agreed that Fichtean idealism was not successful in its attempt to discover absolute knowledge, falling, as it did, into "the abyss of nothingness," he nevertheless believed that "out of this nothing and pure night of infinity, out of the secret abyss that is its birthplace, the truth lifts itself upward."[7] Nihilism, he thought, was "the task of philosophy,"[8] because out of nihilism could come absolute truth. His opinion on this particular point was not widely shared; not surprisingly, he was soon charged with falling victim to nihilism himself by Chr. Weisse in *Die Idee der Gottheit* (1833). The attack on idealism was extended to the literary realm by Jean Paul, who, in his *Vorschule der Aesthetik*, attacked as "poetic nihilism" the romantic fascination with the privacy of individual consciousness.[9] In sum, the earliest discussion of nihilism used the term to signify the loss or dissolution of an independently existing world external to consciousness; in Hegel's words, it referred to the absolute nothing. Almost without exception, nihilism was deemed something best to avoid, the charge "nihilist" serving as a rebuke or a reproach.[10]

If in the first half of the nineteenth century nihilism was linked to the emergence of a particular intellectual movement—idealism, in either its philosophical or poetic form—in the second half nihilism tended to be linked to moral, religious, and political anarchism, usually grounded in loss of belief in God. (The negative polemical connotations of the earlier usage remained.) This association was due in part to Nietzsche—whose works contained references to nihilism throughout the 1880s—but probably entered the popular consciousness through the activities of a group of Russian political dissidents who labeled themselves "nihilists," and the presentation of their views in the novels of Dostoyevsky and Turgenev. Dostoyevsky's *The Possessed* (sometimes translated *The Devils*) describes the activities of a group of nihilists and contains a chilling line of reasoning by one protagonist, Kirolov, that the purest exercise of free will is suicide. (Kirolov eventually proved himself equal to his reasoning.) Turgenev's *Fathers and Sons* describes the conflict between the old and the new generations and offered what was probably the most widely known definition of a nihilist in the late nineteenth century: "a nihilist is a man who...looks at everything critically,...who does not take any principle for granted, however much that principle may be revered."[11] While the definition of nihilist here is positive—and the Russian nihilists themselves used the term with pride[12]—the characterization they received in *Fathers and Sons* was not generally seen as favorable, and the work served to reinforce nihilism's negative cast.[13]

Nietzsche, of course, wrote more explicitly about nihilism than any other nineteenth-century figure; his understanding of nihilism has been the decisive influence on twentieth-century usage. Unfortunately, Nietzsche was ambiguous, vague, and not entirely consistent in his usage of the term; this legacy was transmitted, so that much twentieth-century discussion is also ambiguous, vague, or inconsistent. What Nietzsche began, Heidegger furthered; for Heidegger, nihilism is "forgetfulness of Being," a product of the metaphysical assumptions of the Platonic tradition, now embedded in our language. Heidegger effectively created a new vocabulary for talking about the world and human activity in it, with the result that his discussion of nihilism is highly idiosyncratic and self-consciously non-philosophical.[14]

The problem of nihilism has received a fair amount of attention throughout the twentieth century, but the diverse efforts to analyze and understand it have remained largely isolated from one another. There is no real tradition of literature on nihilism, nor is there unanimity about how nihilism should be defined.

Ernst Juenger has suggested that the lack of a definition is part of the problem, writing that to discover "a good definition of nihilism would be comparable to revealing the cause of cancer."[15] Consider the following range of definitions: Rosen says that "nihilism may be defined as the view that it makes no difference what we say, because every definition of 'difference' is itself merely something that we say."[16] Helmut Thielecke defines nihilism as "the separation of the world from its absolute relation to God," thereby engendering a loss of the self,[17] while Karl Loewith understands it, at least in part, "as the disavowal of existing civilization."[18] Charles Glicksberg notes that "nihilism is difficult to define because it takes so many different forms" but suggests nonetheless that "the nihilist comes to believe that life is a senseless nightmare, a thing of sound and fury signifying nothing, and then struggles desperately to prove that his reasoning or intuition is all wrong."[19] "Absolute nihilism," wrote Camus, is marked by a radical "indifference to life" that leads readily to logical murder.[20] Goudsblom uses nihilism to refer to "a state of mind in which nothing appears to have value or meaning."[21] Peter Unger analyzes "radical nihilism" as the claim that "none of the things which, it seems, are most commonly alleged to exist do in fact exist."[22]

Because of the wide variety of usages "nihilism" has had historically and can have conceptually, it is important to disentangle and clarify the various layers of this notion. This is all the more important since part of my claim in the present work is that the meaning of nihilism has shifted in the last century. The conceptual layering has been modified in ways that are both striking and significant. To put it another way, nihilism is a knot that can be tied in several different ways, with several different threads—the strength of the knot depends on both the way it is tied and what it is tied with. To determine what "nihilism" means in any given case entails determining what strands of nihilism are operative.

Nihilism can be broken down into the following elements, according to the focus of its attack:

1. *Epistemological nihilism* is the denial of the possibility of knowledge. It is sometimes expressed with the claim, "All knowledge claims are equal." Or it may be expressed as, "Every knowledge claim is equally (un)justified." Epistemological nihilists think that no standards exist for distinguishing warranted from unwarranted belief, or knowledge from error. Although similar to skepticism in many regards, there are some important differences. See below, pp. 20–21.

2. *Alethiological nihilism* is the denial of the reality of truth, usually expressed by the claim, "There is no truth." If knowledge is taken to be justified true belief, then alethiological nihilism entails epistemological nihilism; without truth, there can be no knowledge. If, however, knowledge is understood differently (for example, as the beliefs deemed legitimate by a community of discourse), then one can be nihilistic about truth but not about knowledge. (This, I argue below, is the view held by Rorty.) Note that one can hold a theory of truth—an account of what it would take for a proposition to be considered true—and believe that it is impossible to satisfy the necessary conditions (i.e., be an alethiological nihilist.)[23]

3. *Metaphysical or ontological nihilism* is the denial of an (independently existing) world, expressed in the

claim, "Nothing is real." If one holds a correspondence theory of truth, then metaphysical nihilism entails alethiological nihilism; if there is no world for one's beliefs to correspond to or to be about, then no true belief is possible. One could hold a coherence theory of truth, however, and be a metaphysical nihilist, since in coherence theories of truth the world is irrelevant to the truth of belief.[24]

4. *Ethical or moral nihilism* is the denial of the reality of moral or ethical values, expressed in the claim "There is no Good" or "All ethical claims are equally valid." An ethical or moral nihilist does not deny that people use moral or ethical terms; the claim is rather that these terms refer to nothing more than the bias or taste of the assertor.

5. *Existential or axiological nihilism* is the feeling of emptiness and pointlessness that follows from the judgment, "Life has no meaning."[25] As pointed out below, this is probably the most commonplace sense of the word.

While these distinctions will, I believe, prove useful,[26] it is important to remember that in practice, the various senses tend to overlap and intermingle. The belief that there is no truth, for example, has historically been associated with existential nihilism: a world without truth is readily experienced as a world without meaning. For some, ethical nihilism—the denial of the reality of the good—can also lead to existential nihilism. Epistemological nihilism might easily devolve into metaphysical nihilism—if we can't know the world, it might as well not exist. In addition, the distinction between epistemological and alethiological nihilism is not often made, presumably because of the close association between knowledge and truth.

But it is important to distinguish between these various strands, for several reasons. First, as I have already said, the nihilistic knot is not always tied the same way. I will argue below, for example, that the early Karl Barth was an epistemological nihilist, but not an alethiological one. That is, he did not believe that knowledge was possible but he nonetheless held fast to a belief in truth. Richard Rorty, by contrast, is an alethiological nihilist but not an epistemological nihilist. That is, he does not think that truth exists per se, but on his view this does not make our knowledge claims problematic.[27]

One might be tempted to dismiss these distinctions as unnecessarily, even fussily, precise; but the differences between the position of a Barth and the position of a Rorty (or, more generally, between epistemological and alethiological nihilism) are not purely academic. Disentangling the various senses of nihilism is important, second, because the implications of the position are different in each case. Alethiological nihilism, for example, if viewed as a philosophical position about truth, is self-contradictory; epistemological nihilism and ethical nihilism are not.[28] More important, as I will argue in Chapter Six, alethiological nihilism ultimately culminates in its opposite: dogmatism. Epistemological nihilism, in at least some of its forms, does not.

These distinctions are helpful for another reason as well. They enable us to sound out a change in the interpretation of nihilism which it is part of the goal of this work to point out and to characterize. Many of us might be tempted to regard existential nihilism—the view that life is without purpose or meaning—as its principal form, and with good reason. Literary discussions of nihilism (for example, in the works of Dostoyevsky and Camus) tend to focus on this aspect. Nietzsche himself, as we will see, appears chiefly preoccupied with this form. This use of the term is also reinforced by the popular press. If a movie or book is deemed "nihilistic," we know that the hero or anti-hero will be a grim, cynical figure, with no values and no sense of a wider purpose or point.[29] But to infer from this that existential nihilism is the basic or fundamental form of nihilism is to overlook the fact that the judgment "There is no point to the universe" (and, therefore, the feeling of emptiness that ensues from it) is one that is seen as following from or entailed by some prior judgment—usually about the absence of ethical values in the world, or of the non-existence of God. Existential nihilism, in other words, while the most obvious form or aspect of nihilism, is in fact secondary; it is derived from alethiological, epistemological, or ethical nihilism. It is because we believe there is no truth that we conclude that the world is pointless; it is because we think that knowledge is mere illusion that we describe life as meaningless; it is because we see no moral fabric in the universe that we see our existence as without value. The despair of existential nihilism is parasitic on one of the other logically prior forms. This fact is easy to miss because, historically, the conjunction of existential nihilism with one of the other four forms was made almost automatically, so that almost wherever one found epistemological nihilism, one also found existential nihilism.[30]

One final set of distinctions will prove helpful: between nihilism (in its various forms) and two related positions, skepticism and relativism. The most obvious difference between nihilism and these kissing cousins is that, with very few exceptions, no one wishes to be labelled a "nihilist," while "skeptic" and "relativist" have a much more innocuous ring, at least to most people's ears. But there are more telling, if less obvious, differences as well. Skepticism, in its pure forms, merely expresses doubts about the possibility of knowledge or the reliability of our senses and reasoning faculties. It is quite possible to be a skeptic and a devout religious believer; one simply replaces knowledge with faith. Erasmus wrote, in his response to Luther, that given the fallibility of human knowledge it was best to stay within the confines of tradition and accept the dogma of the church.[31] Nihilism, in any of its forms, is at the opposite pole from skepticism, in so far as it ventures to make a (negative) assertion about the nature of the world. An analogy, perhaps, can help clarify the difference: The skeptic stands in the same relation to the nihilist that the agnostic stands to the atheist. The skeptic or the agnostic withholds judgment, because there is insufficient evidence to support an assertion. There could be a God, but the agnostic simply doesn't know; there could be knowledge, but the skeptic simply isn't sure. On the contrary, the atheist and the nihilist actually make substantial claims.[32]

Nor is nihilism identical with all forms of relativism, a more common pairing. Take, for example, epistemological relativism, the view that knowledge claims are relative to a person or a community. While this might deteriorate into nihilism, it need not; relativism, in other words, does not entail nihilism. One can be a relativist, epistemologically speaking, and yet a realist, metaphysically and alethiologically speaking. (Truth could be seen as the sum of all possible perspectives on an independently existing reality, for example.) For that matter, epistemological relativism does not commit one to epistemological nihilism: One can believe that the process of justification is always relative to a particular context, and so maintain both confidence in justification and a belief in truth. One could also believe that while ethics are contextual, there are some elements common to all ethical frameworks.

Finally, it is worth distinguishing nihilism from atheism, given the analogy between them made above. Despite the assumption made by many late-nineteenth-century figures, atheism does not entail nihilism. To cite just one example, the fourth-century-B.C.E. Confucian thinker, Mencius, was not a theist, but offered an elaborate moral vision of the universe that presumed both the possibility and the actuality of knowledge, truth, and goodness. Nor do most forms of nihilism entail atheism, although they are certainly consistent with it. (I might be an ethical nihilist and a theist, for example, believing that God transcends what human beings call morality, and deeming the latter mere convention.) The only form of nihilism which seems to lead irrevocably to atheism is alethiological nihilism. If there is no truth, there can be no God in any conventional sense of the term.[33]

My principal concern in this work is with three of the five strands of nihilism: epistemological, alethiological, and existential. In particular, I am interested in the connections between them, the associations, both historical and conceptual, that tie them together and, more recently, have broken them apart. Although on my view Nietzsche was primarily concerned with existential nihilism, his discussion often conflates all three forms. Barth maintained the conjunction of existential and epistemological nihilism, but eschewed its alethiological form. Rorty disentangles all three strands, and embraces what Barth (and, I will argue, Nietzsche) rejects.

One final, cautionary note is in order. The typology of nihilism given here might well imply that nihilism is reflectively articulated; as a matter of fact, it almost invariably is not. Although readily associated with certain philosophical stances, nihilism is usually not itself a philosophical position, and it is misleading to view it as such. Nihilism is better described as an outlook or a perspective that underlies the more reflective portions of a thinker's overall view. Neither Barth nor Rorty (or, for that matter, Nietzsche) identified himself as a nihilist in any of its variants, nor does either offer an intellectual defense of nihilism. Nonetheless, the position of each is knotted with distinctively nihilistic threads. The task of the present work is, in part, to disentangle these knots.

Part II

Nihilism and Crisis

3

Nietzsche and the Crisis of Nihilism

THE NATURE OF NIETZSCHE'S CONCERN WITH NIHILISM

In a fragment from early in 1888, entitled "Nihilism—for the preface," Nietzsche wrote:

> Until now I have endured a torture: all of the laws by which life unfolds appeared to me to be in opposition to the values for the sake of which we endure life. This does not appear to be a condition from which many consciously suffer; nonetheless I intend to gather together the signs from which I take it to be the fundamental character and the really tragic problem of our modern world, and as concealed necessity, the cause or interpretation of all of its needs. This problem has become conscious in me. (KSA 12:7 [8])

One of the many sketches found after his death, this fragment clearly shows Nietzsche's conviction both of the magnitude of the problem of nihilism and the significance of his own role in its history. Characteristically, the note portrays nihilism as a condition of tension, as a disproportion between what we want to value (or need) and how the world appears to operate. Nihilism, the "pathos of the 'in vain' (*umsonst*)" (KSA 12:9 [60]), is the "antagonism, not to esteem what we know, no longer to be allowed to esteem the lies we would like to tell ourselves" (KSA 12:5

[71], WP:55). Our pessimism is precisely this: "The world is not worth what we believed—our faith itself has so intensified [*gesteigert*] our drive to knowledge that today we must say this" (KSA 12:6 [25]).

Nietzsche's analysis of nihilism as the self-dissolution of the will to truth, of "truth at any price" is well known, and despite the fact that his discussion of nihilism is restricted almost entirely to his notebooks, few scholars fail to accord his treatment of it a prominent role in his thought.[1] Because of this prominence it may seem unnecessary or even frivolous to ask why Nietzsche was concerned with nihilism in the first place. The answer seems obvious. We might say that Nietzsche was concerned with nihilism because he was concerned with Christian morality, and nihilism was, on his analysis, not only the logical but the necessary consequence of that value system (see KSA 13:13 [4], 13:11 [411]; WP:Preface). Or we might link his concerns to his self-image as an acute cultural critic, and say that he was interested in nihilism as the characteristic but largely unacknowledged temper of his day, as the opening quotation suggests. Or again, we might say that he was driven to consider it given the nihilistic bent of many of his own views, for example, his oft-stated conviction that there is no truth, or his myth of the Eternal Recurrence.

Certainly none of these answers is wrong. Nietzsche was indeed profoundly interested in Christian morality, the mechanisms by which it operated, as well as its relation to what he perceived to be the spiritual decline of his age, nor can one deny that he delighted in talking about the impossibility of truth and the pointlessness of the world without God. Yet to view nihilism as essentially an offshoot of other, more basic concerns belies the increasingly central role that the analysis of nihilism plays in his notebooks from 1886 on, and oversimplifies an admittedly confusing, and perhaps confused, array of fragments.

To attempt to sort out what Nietzsche meant by nihilism is to confront a tangle of issues that must be teased out with great delicacy. Nietzsche used the word "nihilism" in a variety of ways, many of which are in tension with one another.[2] Nihilism is described as an historical process, a psychological state, a philosophical position, a cultural condition, a sign of weakness, a sign of strength, as the danger of dangers, and as a divine way of thinking.[3] Reviewing this dizzying spectrum may leave one with the feeling that the only clear thing Nietzsche ever said about nihilism was that it is ambiguous. But even this is undermined by his frequently dogmatic pronouncements about it.

Fortunately we know that Nietzsche's notebooks were filled with philosophical experiments; what one finds in them are attempts to lay out his thoughts, to discover the perfect turn of phrase, the most provocative argument, the most efficient approach. They range in kind from very polished sketches that are often virtually indistinguishable from the final, published version to cryptic notes such as that made so much of by Derrida: "'Ich habe meinen Regenschirm vergessen'."[4] Many of them were never intended to be published in any form at all, simply the private thoughts of an overfull mind. On the one hand, this makes our task harder, or perhaps impossible, for by what criteria do we pick and choose among the fragments to separate the "real Nietzsche" from the "unreal"? On the other hand, it invites us to ourselves experiment, to share in Nietzsche's thoughts not by recreating them exactly as he himself thought them—clearly an impossible task, with any text—but by exploring the possibilities inherent in them, given what we can claim to know about his views with some modicum of confidence.[5]

So we must ask ourselves, why was Nietzsche concerned with nihilism? What common threads run through these fragments, from which we can weave, if not Nietzsche's own pattern, then one which is compatible with his thought taken as a whole? First, and perhaps most important, nihilism is almost always linked to interpretation, in one of three ways. Nihilism is used to describe (1) particular negating, life-denying interpretations of the world, such as Buddhism or Christianity; (2) the absence of any meaningful interpretation of the world, usually due to the collapse of the prevailing interpretation; (3) the multiplicity of possible interpretations, all deemed equally false, ("the denial of a truthful world": KSA 12:9 [41], WP:15). This constant juxtaposition of nihilism and interpretation suggests that we must understand Nietzsche's analysis of nihilism within the context of his portrayal of man as *homo hermeneuticus,* as an organism that invariably and necessarily interprets.

Second, nihilism is usually linked to sickness, decay, disintegration. Nihilism, Nietzsche wrote, is "the expression of physiological decadence," its "logical result" (KSA 13: 17 [8], WP: 38, 43). Yet this does not mean that it is therefore an essentially negative phenomenon for Nietzsche. Disease, degeneration, decadence are ambiguous phenomena for Nietzsche, conditions that can culminate in dissolution and death but can also result in increase and improvement. "Waste, decay, elimination need not be condemned; they are necessary consequences of life, of the growth of life.... Decadence is as necessary as any increase and advance of life" (KSA 13:14 [75], WP:40). There are diseases from which one returns healthier, stronger than before, as Nietzsche suggested in the preface to *The Gay Science;* some diseases are in fact necessary for health. This explains why nihilism can be either a symptom of strength, of a spirit so vigorous it imposes its will through the destruction and annihilation of its surroundings, or of weakness, of a spirit too exhausted to do more than passively succumb to the emptiness that threatens to engulf it (see KSA 12:9 [35], WP:22, 23). Nietzsche believed that "health and sickness are not essentially different...only degree differentiates both kinds of existence: The exaggeration, the disproportion, the non-harmony constitutes the sickly state" (KSA 12:14 [65]; cf. WP:47). Consequently, nihilism, too, differs from a condition of normality, of health, only through the "pathological generalization" of its suspicion and disbelief.

These two facts—that nihilism is usually linked on the one hand to interpretation, on the other hand to sickness and disease—indicate that we should think of nihilism as a hermeneutical malaise, as some sort of breakdown or dysfunction in the interpretive processes that comprise human life. This also sheds light on why the problem of nihilism preoccupied Nietzsche as much as it did: His interest in interpretation, in the interpretive quality of all human behavior, inevitably drove him to consider aberrations as part of this process. Not only would his vision of man afford him a unique and penetrating angle in the analysis of nihilism, but an examination of aberrant forms of interpretation would provide new insights for the understanding of normal and healthy forms.[6]

For Nietzsche, in other words, nihilism primarily refers to the loss of meaning that follows from interpretive paralysis. The principal and most frequent sense in which he used the term was to refer to axiological or existential nihilism. Nietzsche recognized, of course, that existential nihilism is not born in a vaccuum; as we shall see, he offered a sustained and penetrating account of the historical preconditions of the—in his eyes—growing hermeneutical disease. Nonetheless, the form of nihilism which chiefly preoccuppied him was the absence of meaning, a condition he saw as brought on by recognizing the falseness of the Platonic-Christian paradigm.

In order to understand both the ways in which nihilism afflicts or distorts the interpretive process of an individual (or a community, or a culture), as well as why the distortion of this process was the cause of such concern to Nietzsche, we must first have some idea of the role Nietzsche attributes to interpretation in human life. We must, in other words, first come to grips with the problem of interpretation in Nietzsche's thought before we can examine the ways in which interpretation becomes a problem.

HUMAN INTERPRETATION AND THE DEMAND FOR MEANING

Recent studies on Nietzsche have done a great deal to sensitize his readers to the radical epistemic perspectivism of his thought, as well as the corresponding emphasis on interpretation as inseparable from life.[7] While most of these analyses rely heavily upon the *Nachgelassene Fragmente* to develop their arguments, there is sufficient support within the published corpus to warrant the claim that Nietzsche took his perspectivism very seriously indeed, and that interpretation (*Auslegung*) was a central concept in his thinking from the very beginning. His earliest notebook entries probed the relationships between art, metaphysics, religion, and science as various perspectives on and interpretations of the world, while later entries called for *"Auslegung, nicht Erklarung"* ("interpretation, not explanation") as the task of reflection (KSA 12:2 [85]). His rejection of Kant's noumenal world, of the Platonic realm of ideas, of the Christian's "true world," became one of the driving themes of his published works. But, unlike many of his contemporaries, he did not replace the idealism shared by Kant, Plato, and (in Nietzsche's eyes) Paul with a positivistic phenomenalism or materialism. He wrote:

> Against the positivism that halts at phenomena—"There are only facts"—I would say no, facts are precisely what there are not, only interpretations. We can establish no fact "in itself"; perhaps it is foolishness to want such a thing. (KSA 12:7 [60], WP:481)

All we have access to, Nietzsche asserted, are interpretations of the world. We have no access to the world as it "really" is. This thought, of course, is hardly original with Nietzsche; it was precisely the impetus behind Kant's "Copernican Revolution." Yet Nietzsche's analysis of this situation differs significantly from Kant's, for Nietzsche wanted to undermine the concept of the noumenon (the "thing-in-itself") by stressing the relational nature of knowledge. Knowledge—or more exactly, what we call "knowledge"—is always the knowledge of something by someone (KSA 13:14 [22]). Our access to the world is always mediated by our minds and our bodies; perception itself is, strictly speaking, interpretation, in that it necessarily modifies and changes what is "out there" to suit our needs.

This is all well and good—but Nietzsche went further still. The passage continues:

> "Everything is subjective," you say; but already this is interpretation. The subject is nothing given; rather it is something invented, stuck behind [the interpretation]. Is it ultimately necessary to put an interpreter behind the interpretation? Already this is invention (*Dichtung*), hypothesis.

Hence any attempt to ground interpretation in some point of origin is already to commit oneself to a particular interpretation.

Yet it would be a mistake if we were to infer from this that we are, like Cratylus, merely to sit in a corner and wag our finger because there is nothing we can say with any certainty of meaning about the world. Nietzsche was far from trying to advocate skeptical detachment or disengagement from the world. In fact, this is precisely the kind of response he wished to avoid, a response he regarded as the negative form of nihilism. He asked not that we stop interpreting—something which would only be possible with our death—but only that we recognize any particular interpretive act for what it is, namely, an interpretation, one of many that are possible. The passage continues,

> So far generally as the word "knowledge" has meaning, the world is knowable, but it is interpretable otherwise. It has no [one] meaning behind it, rather, countless meanings. "Perspectivism."

With this brief sentence Nietzsche captured the essence of his philosophical perspectivism. It is not to be understood as a denial of either meaning or of knowledge *per se*, only as a denial that there is any one meaning undergirding the world as it is in and of itself. Put positively, Nietzsche's perspectivism asserted that there are as many interpretations of the world—in a practical sense, as many worlds—as there are perspectives on it.

The perspective we have on the world is largely a function of the (mostly unconscious) needs and desires that motivate us to act. To continue our passage:

> It is our needs that interpret the world: our drives and their For and Against. Every drive is a kind of lust to rule, each has its perspective, which it would force upon all other drives as a norm.

Nietzsche's appeal to "drives" (*Trieb,* often translated as "instinct") is of course open to the charge of being mere interpretation itself. Yet such a charge would not faze him. On the one hand, if everything is interpretation, there is no longer any sense to the phrase "mere interpretation." The accusation has lost its sting—even, to a large extent, its descriptive power. On the other hand, Nietzsche's lengthy analysis of human beings as complexes of drives in, for example, *Daybreak,* can easily be seen as serving an heuristic and not a descriptive function. He had no interest, à la Freud, in systematizing into a coherent set the body of drives that comprise an individual, nor did he think, finally, that it is even possible to do so, given their complete and intrinsic inaccessibility to us. Rather, his analysis of humans in terms of drives was part of his attempt to undermine even our sense of self, our conviction that through self-knowledge, at least, we can find a legitimate basis upon which to ground our thoughts. We are as enigmatic to ourselves as is the world.[8]

Nietzsche's position may seem dangerously close to a kind of universal solipsism, wherein each individual lives in a world completely of his or her own making. But his understanding of perspectivism is not as individualistic as the foregoing account perhaps suggests, since he clearly recognized the intersubjective nature of the world in which we live. Predictably, Nietzsche analyzed this shared world in terms of the drives and needs he postulated as common to all human beings, those that make them human and enable them to survive as humans.

The motive behind the development of our organs of knowledge, according to Nietzsche, is the preservation and maintenance of the human species. "The organs of knowledge...develop in such a way that their observations suffice for our preservation" (KSA 13:14 [122], WP:480). The very things we perceive, the objects of our knowledge, as well as the manner in which we perceive them, are constrained and determined by the utility of such perceptions. Nietzsche wrote that "the measure of that [of] which we are in any way conscious is dependent upon the coarse utility of its becoming conscious" (KSA 13:11 [120], WP:474). In other words, we perceive only what we need to perceive in order to survive. Likewise, we know only what we need to know to continue flourishing as a species: "It is improbable that our 'knowledge' should extend further than is strictly necessary for the preservation of life" (KSA 11:36 [19], WP:494). Consciousness itself is, in Nietzsche's eyes, present only to the extent that it is useful for it to be present (KSA 12:2 [95], WP:505): "Even our intellect is a consequence of conditions of existence—: We would not have it *as it is* if we could live *otherwise*" (KSA 11:26 [137], WP:498). That we have knowledge of the world at all, as well as the particular kind of knowledge that we have, is a function of our need for it in order to survive as a species.

But why do we need knowledge in order to survive? Nietzsche wrote, "In order for a particular species to maintain itself and increase its power, its conception of reality must comprehend enough of the calculable and constant for it to base a scheme of behavior on it" (KSA 13:14 [122], WP:480). The suggestion is that our knowledge, such as it is, is necessary for our survival, because it provides us with a basis for interacting with and, in particular, taking control of, our environment. Knowledge "works as a tool of power" (KSA 13:14 [122], WP:480).

Consequently, our attempts to know the world are comparable to an amoeba's incorporation of external material (KSA 12:5 [65], WP:501) or a protoplasm's appropriation of foreign objects (KSA 12:7 [9], WP:510). "Knowledge" is to be understood as a "taking possession of things" (KSA 11:26 [61], WP:503), "understanding," as the ability to "express something new in the language of something old and familiar" (KSA 13:15 [90], WP:479), "thinking" as "fitting new material into old schemas...*making* equal what is new" (KSA 11:41 [11], WP:499).

Knowledge, thus described, is fundamentally a levelling process, an assimilation and domestication of what is novel, foreign, inexplicable. The implicit premise of Nietzsche's discussion is that in order to survive, an organism must be able to cope with what is unfamiliar and unexplained by subsuming it under the categories of the familiar and the understood. Our knowing process does this by explaining new phenomena in terms of the old, by carving corners off square pegs, as it were, forcing them into the round holes that we find more manageable. Nietzsche's claim that knowledge is a "*making* equal of what is new" should be stressed, for, according to his view, we create reality, forcing it into a form that suits our needs and enables us to live in it (KSA 12:9 [97], WP:516). Knowledge must be consistent with our "need for security, for quick understanding on the basis of signs and sounds" (KSA 12:6 [11], WP:513).

As a result, Nietzsche claimed, "our apparatus for acquiring knowledge is not designed for 'knowledge'," if by "knowledge" we mean the disinterested mirroring of reality, the portrayal of the world as it is. The goal of thinking is "not 'to know' but to schematize—to impose upon chaos as much regularity and form as our practical needs require" (KSA 13:14 [152], WP:515). What we call "knowledge" is an expression, not of truth, but of our basic survival needs as a species. We have no way of evaluating the efficacy of our epistemic process in gaining truth, for we have no access to the objects of knowledge other than the process itself.

> One would have to know what *being* is in order to decide whether this or that is real; in the same way, what *certain-*

> *ty* is, what *knowledge* is, and the like. But since we do not know this, a critique of the faculty of knowledge is senseless: how should a tool be able to criticize itself when it can only use itself as a critique?" (KSA 12:2 [87], WP:486)

Nonetheless, Nietzsche appeared to feel justified in calling all of our basic concepts "fictions," fictions apparently because they reify and make static a world which is in a continual state of flux. He noted, "A world in a state of becoming could not, in a strict sense, be 'comprehended' or 'known'" (KSA 11:36 [23], WP:520). We necessarily impose static and fixed concepts onto experience, in order to understand and manipulate it. Logic demands that the world be constituted by essentially unchanging entities that interact in a constant, regular fashion. "In order to think and infer it is necessary to assume beings: logic handles only formulas for what remains the same" (KSA 13:9, WP:517). Or again, "Knowledge is possible only on the basis of belief in being" (KSA 12:2 [91], WP:518). We have no choice in this matter; it could not possibly be otherwise, because we cannot divorce thought and language, understood as a logically structured pattern of concepts. "We *think* only in the form of language.... We cease to think when we refuse to do so under the constraint of language" (KSA 12:5 [22], WP:522). We are committed—or condemned, depending on one's point of view—to the rational falsification of the world. "Rational thought is interpretation according to a scheme we cannot throw off" (KSA 12:5 [22], WP:522).

We create a complex of mental constructs and thrust it upon the world; only in this way is knowledge, or rather, what we call knowledge, possible. Where, though, does this complex of concepts come from? How do concepts originate? Nietzsche offered no transcendental (or, for that matter, immanential) deduction of the categories, no fully worked out theory of their origin. Three things, however, may safely be said. First, all of our basic concepts—substance, accident, doer, deed, causality, even truth and reality—stem from our belief in the ego. Nietzsche asserted this in several places (KSA 13:10 [19], WP:485; KSA 13:9 [98], WP:488; WP:483), without explaining the derivation in any detail. Second, belief in the ego arises out of the conventions of language. "That when there is thought there has to be something 'that thinks' is simply a function of our grammatical custom that adds a doer to every deed" (KSA 12:10 [158], WP:484; see also KSA 8:38 [3]).[9] Third, the ego and its derivative concepts were elevated to the status of *a priori* truths because of their utility and expediency relative to a certain species (KSA 14:14 [105], WP:514). Thus our basic categories of thought are simply tools we use to apprehend and manipulate the world, a function of our perspective, our habits, and our needs. Unreflectively, we assume that they capture and express the nature of things when in truth they are merely an expression of our inability to conceive of things in any other way.

That we are locked into this one way of conceptualizing the world seems at many times to be Nietzsche's position, largely because we cannot choose to disbelieve in the ego. "Our thinking itself involves this belief [in the ego] (with its distinctions of substance, accident, deed, doer, etc.); to let it go means: being no longer able to think" (WP:487). Yet at other times he suggested that alternative interpretations or conceptualizations of the world are indeed possible for us, not only in theory, but in practice. He toyed with the idea, for example, of replacing belief in a single subject, the ego, with belief in a hierarchy of subjects, presumably the various drives within the individual that seek satisfaction.

> The assumption of one single subject is perhaps unnecessary; perhaps it is just as permissable to assume a multiplicity of subjects, whose interaction and struggle is the basis of our thought and our consciousness in general?... *My hypothesis*, the subject as multiplicity. (KSA 11:40 [42], WP:490)[10]

Thus Nietzsche's epistemological stance stresses, on the one hand, the relativity of knowledge to the demands and needs of the knower: The very delineation of the object of knowledge is a function of how the knower is by nature constituted. On the other hand, it also stresses the species-specific nature of the fundamental categories we use to organize the world. Because we have the same sorts of sense organs, shared language patterns, and a common need to become master of our surroundings (in order to survive, if for no other reason), the phenomenal world in which we live—the objects and events that we see—is essentially a shared one.

The particular valuations we give to these objects and events, however, vary among us. Different individuals have different needs, and like-minded individuals naturally form communities that reinforce and stabilize the valuations of the individuals, as well as raising future generations to conform to these valuations. Morality is, according to Nietzsche, one of the fundamental ways communities interpret and make sense of (i.e., give meaning to) their environment and their own actions and thoughts. His by now classic analysis of master and slave moralities in *On the Genealogy of Morals* fleshes out his conviction that moralities "are a sign-language of the affects." By looking at what people value, at the order of rank they apply to the world, one learns not only how they understand the world and their own place in it but what instincts are dominant in a community or an individual.

Nietzsche's analysis of the various types of interpretations and the ways they operate is fascinating, but what is important for our present purpose is Nietzsche's insistence that we all inevitably, necessarily interpret the world, either by imposing our will on our surroundings or, more commonly, by accepting and participating in the will of a community. Nietzsche distinguished in a preliminary fashion between strong, healthy evaluations (which frankly take their origin in an individual or group that defines its own existence positively) and weak, sick evaluations, (which originate in reaction to something external, and generally define the existence of the group or individual negatively.) The most extreme forms of weakness do not acknowledge the internal origin of their evaluation, giving it an objective, independent status.[11] "He who does not know how to lay his will in things at least attributes a meaning to them: That means he believes a will already is in them."[12] The origin of this belief, of course, is the individual or the community, but the weakest individuals and groups lack the strength to accept the knowledge that they are creating and imposing the meaning themselves.[13] The important thing—the goal, and perhaps motivation, of interpretation—is that there is meaning, be it "found" or implanted.

Consequently nihilism, described by Nietzsche as "absolute valuelessness" (KSA 12:9 [1]), as the conviction that *"Alles hat keinen Sinn"* ("Nothing has meaning"; see KSA 12:2 [109]) and of "the meaninglessness of events" (KSA 12:2 [109]), is *"die Gefahr der Gefahren"* ("the danger of dangers; see KSA 12:2 [100, 118, 129]). Why is it so dangerous? Because it is through valuation, through the imposition of meaning, that people survive. The attribution of meaning enables us to endure life, to suffer dire and painful occurrences. We are constitutionally built to interpret, to impose our meaning and our will on our surroundings. To will no longer, to suffer existence merely passively without offering some sort of interpretation, explanation, or justification, signifies the ultimate degeneration of an organism, the final decay of its instinctual nature into nothingness, a degeneration and decay that, left unchecked, can only culminate in the death of that organism.

THE ADVENT OF THE "UNCANNIEST OF ALL GUESTS"

Nietzsche found signs of this condition everywhere around him, although the progress of nihilism was, in late nineteenth century Europe, still incomplete (KSA 12:10 [142], WP:19, 28). Nor was he alone in his somewhat grim diagnosis of the future of European culture or in his conviction that contemporary decadence must be linked to the death of God.[14] Unique to Nietzsche's analysis, however, was his realization that not only is God dead (that is, there no longer exists a center, a ground, a foundational point in our lives), but, "We have killed him" (that is, that this situation is a consequence of our efforts to establish and certify such a ground).[15] The well-known parable of the madman in *The Gay Science* (III, 125) expresses in allegorical form Nietzsche's account of the self-dissolution of the truth imperative of Platonic-Christianity.[16]

Nietzsche regarded the contemporary onslaught of meaninglessness, of the *umsonst*, as a direct consequence of the collapse of the Christian moral interpretation of the world, a collapse brought about by the consistent application of its own moral hierarchy. The will to truth, fostered by Christianity above all else as the means whereby one acquires the proper relationship to the divine, ultimately turns against the metaphysical framework that made it intelligible, showing it to be false and untenable. Nietzsche put it succinctly thus:

> But among the forces cultivated by morality was *truthfulness*: This eventually turned against morality, discovered its interested perspective—and now the recognition of this inveterate mendaciousness that one despairs of shedding becomes a stimulant. To nihilism. Now we discover in ourselves needs implanted by centuries of moral interpretation—needs that now appear to us as needs for untruth; on the other hand, the value for which we endure life seems to hinge upon these needs. This antagonism—not to esteem what we know, not to be allowed any longer to esteem the lies we should like to tell ourselves—results in a process of dissolution. (KSA 12:5 [71]; cf. WP:5)

We must not overlook the irony of this situation. It is precisely Christian piety that demands that we give up Christianity; it is our commitment to the truth that compels us to admit that our concept of God is a lie.[17] The brilliance of Nietzsche's dissection of contemporary nihilism lies in his recognition that nihilism is not due to Christian apostasy, to a deliberate turning one's back on one's heritage, but is the result of the sincere and consistent application of Christian values:

> We are no longer Christians; we outgrew Christianity, not because we lived too far from it, rather because we lived too close, even more because we grew [i.e., developed] out of it. It is our strict and over-indulged piety itself that today forbids us still to be Christians. (KSA 12:2 [200])

It is not that we are no longer motivated by the Platonic-Christian paradigm—Nietzsche himself said that he draws his flame from the same fire that burned in Socrates[18]—but that we have witnessed the persistent erosion of the context which made that framework intelligible and coherent. The history of philosophy in the West is "the history of the development of the will to truth," culminating in the will-to-truth's "putting itself in question" (*Selbst-in-Fragestellung*) (KSA 12:9 [1]).

This event, though potentially cataclysmic in its conseqences, is occurring slowly, and is not fully seen or understood: "This tremendous event is still on its way; even yet it has not reached the ears of men.... Deeds, although done, still require time to be seen and heard" (*Gay Science* III, 125). And while, intellectually, we might recognize the illegitimacy and untenability of many aspects of the Platonic-Christian tradition, we nonetheless still have the sorts of needs and questions that it fulfilled and answered. It bred us to have these needs, and while they may be as suspect as the fulfillment historically provided, the needs remain. Such is our pathos:

> But the tragic thing is that we can no longer *believe* those dogmas of religion and metaphysics, once we have the rigorous method of truth in our hearts and heads, and yet on the other hand, the development of mankind has made us so delicate, sensitive, and ailing that we need the most potent kinds of cures and comforts—hence arises the need that man might bleed to death from the truth he has recognized.[19]

Despite the many criticisms Nietzsche levied at Christianity—for example, that its clear promotion of humility and meekness fosters a weak, degenerate type of human being—he recognized the important role it has played in human history as an interpretation providing meaning. While contemporary nihilism was, in Nietzsche's eyes, a direct consequence of the radical dissolution of Christianity, Christianity itself arose in response to nihilism. Christian morality, he remarked, "was the great antidote against practical and theoretical nihilism" in that it "protected life against despair and the leap into nothing" among the underprivileged, the disenfranchised, the powerless (KSA 12:5 [71], WP:55). It did so by "assigning to each an infinite value, a metaphysical value" and postulating the existence of a world where the perceived inequalities of the present were reversed (KSA 12:5 [71], WP:55). Most important, perhaps, it made evil and suffering appear "full of meaning" and "prevented man from despising himself as man" (KSA 12:5 [71], WP:4). The world was seen as having significance and purpose, and a significance and a purpose that were not only intelligible to human beings but that also accorded them a prominent role in its hierarchy.

In contrast to this, "the most universal sign of the modern age" is that "man has *lost* dignity in his own eyes to an incredible extent" (KSA 12:7 [3], WP:18). Not only has he lost his exalted place in the world order, but his ability to understand his surroundings, to discover the truth about things, has been undermined as well. And with the dissolution of a centuries-old theodical structure, we find that "the time has come when we must pay for having been Christians for two thousand years: We are losing the center of gravity that allows us to live; we are lost for a time." The immediate consequence of this is that "we plunge abruptly into the opposite valuations with the same measure of energy with which we were Christians" (KSA 13:11 [148], WP:30). This is "psychologically necessary," according to Nietzsche, since the collapse of the prevailing interpretation, when it has been taken to be absolute truth, naturally leads to a distrust of all meanings: "One interpretation has collapsed; but because it was considered *the* interpretation, it now seems as if there were no meaning at all in existence, as though everything were in vain" (KSA 12:5 [71], WP:55).

Despite its necessity, Nietzsche found "the inference that there is no meaning at all" to be a "tremendous generalization" that was "pathological" in being so extreme (KSA 12:9 [35], WP:13). While he acknowledged that "the world is not worth what we believed," he suggested that, far from having no meaning, "the world could be worth much more than we believed" (KSA 12:6 [25], WP:32). This fact is hidden to us because of the absoluteness of the Christian claim to a monopoly on truth and its repudiation of all other accounts of life as false or illusory, which prevent us from seeing alternative interpretations with an unjaundiced eye. This very absoluteness contributed to Christianity's demise, according to Nietzsche: "Christianity is broken apart by the unconditional character of its morality" (KSA 12:2 [123]). It sets up a standard for truth that it itself could not ultimately meet, leaving behind only the world of appearance it repudiated. "This supreme disappointment"—of being left with a world we have been taught to disvalue—is added "to the reasons why [the world] deserves to be repudiated" (KSA 12:9 [407], WP:37).

As this condition becomes more pronounced, two responses to it become evident, or rather, two forms of it are likely to develop, one "active," the other "passive." Passive nihilism merely succumbs to the nothingness that surrounds it, being essentially an expression of weakness. "The power of the spirit can be so worn down that the previous aims and values are inadequate and it [can] find no more faith." It is unable to "posit for itself, productively, a goal, a why, a faith" (KSA 12:9 [35]). Active nihilism, in contrast, is a sign of strength; here, too, the previous aims and values are found to be inadequate, but this is because the spirit has grown too rich, too full to find them an appropriate channel for its needs and instincts.

Analogously, Nietzsche distinguished between two states that he stressed were "not to be confused—lack of faith as a general inability to believe and, on the other side, [lack of faith] as inability to continue to believe something in particular. The last case [is] commonly a symptom of a new faith" (KSA 13:11 [106]). The first type of loss of faith, the general inability to believe, "is peculiar to the incapacity to negate—it does not know how to turn itself against either a yes or a no" (KSA 13:11 [106]). It lacks the strength to resist anything, ultimately being too enfeebled to respond. Destruction is necessary for life, however; not only is it needed to create but also in order to mold one's surroundings to conform to one's will. Destruction, predictably, is a typical aspect of active nihilism.[20]

This does not mean, however, that passive nihilism is a form of sickness while active nihilism is a form of health; both are, in Nietzsche's eyes, instances of disease, for both are pathologically extreme in their actions. Yet Nietzsche suggested that active nihilism is a disease that at a certain point is to be sought, in some sense at least, for the benefits that convalescing from it has to offer. Despite the frequently apocalyptic tenor of Nietzsche's pronouncements about nihilism, he viewed its arrival as potentially a good thing:

> I praise, I do not reproach, its arrival. I believe it is one of the greatest crises, a moment of the deepest self-reflection of humanity. Whether man recovers from it, whether he becomes master of this crisis, is a question of his strength. It is possible.... (KSA 13:11 [119])

NIHILISM: DISEASE OR CURE?

To appreciate the potentially restorative effects of the nihilistic malaise, it is useful to examine Nietzsche's own recovery from this illness. Nietzsche—or at least, the image Nietzsche sought to convey in his published works[21]—can be seen as regarding himself as living through, in microcosmic form, the history of the next two centuries. In 1887/88 he described himself as "the first perfect nihilist of Europe who, however, has even now lived through the whole of nihilism, to the end, leaving it behind, outside himself" (KSA 12:11 [411], WP:Preface, 3; see also KSA 12:9 [123]). For him, at least, the recognition that there is no undergirding meaning or truth to the universe, no divine purpose behind the world was *"die grosse Befreiung"* ("the great liberation"), that brought out *"die Unschuld des Werdens"* ("the innocence of becoming"). The denial of God, of God's responsibility for the world "redeems" (*erloesen*) the world.[22]

Such a cure and the corresponding redemption are not necessarily Nietzsche's unique possession. He wrote,

> A philosopher heals himself differently [than others]; he heals himself, for example, through nihilism. The belief that there is no truth, the nihilist belief, is a great stretching of the limbs for one who, as a warrior of knowledge, incessantly lies in battle with hateful truths. For truth is hateful. (KSA 13:11 [108])

Note that here, strictly speaking, Nietzsche is referring not to existential nihilism, but rather to alethiological nihilism or, perhaps, to epistemological nihilism.[23] Nihilism, he stated, is "our kind of laziness" (KSA 13:16 [30]). The belief that there is no truth, in other words, paradoxically can serve as a respite in the search for truth, a catharsis of sorts, leading to stronger, healthier states.

The curious dialectic of health and sickness of which we spoke earlier—that sickness can be a means to health—is more fully played out in a series of prefaces Nietzsche wrote between 1886 and 1888. In most, if not all, of the prefaces Nietzsche wrote during this time (either to newly published works or to second editions) some mention is made of convalescence, usually of Nietzsche's alone. And in the prefaces to *Human, All-too-human* and *The Gay Science* in particular, one finds a subtle interweaving of reflections on sickness convalescence, recovery, gratitude, and health.[24]

The earliest of the prefaces, that of *Human, All-too-human*, was written in the spring of 1886. In eight brief sections (none longer than two pages, most considerably shorter) Nietzsche laid out the development of the "free spirit"—an honorific term describing a higher type of human being who could, arguably, one day redeem Europe's degeneracy. In part autobiographical (he noted in the final section, "No psychologist or soothsayer will have a moment's difficulty in discovering at which place in the development sketched out above the present book belongs"), in part impersonal, the description of the free spirit's path is detailed from an initial "gratitude for the ground out of which they grew,...for the shrine where they learned to worship" through a "morbid isolation" that questions, "Cannot all values be overturned?... Is everything perhaps ultimately false?" to a state of "enormous, overflowing certainty and health" which sees the world "transformed." Thus the free spirit, originally nurtured and educated in a tradition it is taught to revere and love, goes through a transitional period of radical doubt and suspicion, seeking to overthrow not only the values that bred it but all values altogether. This massive suspicion ultimately if mysteriously engenders a renewed appreciation for the world that had been previously devalued. The parallels to nihilism and Nietzsche's proposed transvaluation of values are clear.

The preface opens with an exercise in self-reflection. "Truly," he wrote, "I myself do not believe that anyone has ever looked into the world with such deep suspicion." Such suspicion isolates and wounds; its "chills and fears" require a recovery of some kind. The need for a "cure" and a "restoration" point unambiguously to Nietzsche's identification of this suspicion with illness and disease. The necessary cure, he wrote, was "the belief that I was *not* the only one to be thus, to *see* thus"; necessary for his convalescence was "a shared blindness, with no suspicion or question marks, a pleasure in foregrounds, surfaces, what is near, what is nearest, in everything that has color, skin, appearance." Thus the suspicion that plunges into the depths needs to be followed or tempered, periodically, with a delight in surface, in immediacy. "Such falseness," Nietzsche remarked, is necessary "so that I may keep permitting myself the luxury of my truthfulness." The delight in immediacy is not a final state, an end in itself, but a means, a respite, that enables this indulgence in truth.

Nietzsche acknowledged that it was out of a desire for company, a weariness of solitude and isolation, that the free spirits to whom *Human, All-too-human* was dedicated were invented. Their invention notwithstanding, "I already see them *coming*, slowly, slowly" and he wondered, "Perhaps I am doing something to hasten their coming when I describe before the fact the fateful conditions that I *see* giving rise to them, the paths on which I *see* them coming?"

Necessary for them to "ripen to sweet perfection" is a prior "great separation"—like that suffered by Nietzsche himself through his incessant questioning—an "earthquake," in which "the young soul is devastated, torn lose, torn out." Filled with "horror and suspicion" at what was once loved, the soul is visited with a "violent and dangerous curiosity for an undiscovered world." The old has become too narrow, too constricted for "this first outburst of strength and will to self-determination." In consequence,

> With an evil laugh he overturns what he finds concealed, spared until then by some shame; he investigates how these things look if they are overturned. There is some arbitrariness and pleasure in arbitrariness to it, if he then perhaps directs his favor to that which previously stood in disrepute—if he creeps curiously and enticingly around what is most forbidden. Behind his ranging activity...stands the question mark of an ever more dangerous curiosity. "Cannot *all* values be overturned? And is Good perhaps Evil? And God only an invention, a nicety of the devil? Is everything perhaps ultimately false?

This suspicion that "everything [is] perhaps ultimately false" is linked, in the privacy of his notebooks, to nihilism, nihilism of the most extreme form (KSA 12:9

[41], WP:15). And the free spirit's need to burst free from the past, to negate, to overthrow, parallels the strong spirit's active nihilism in face of old values too decrepit to serve as a catalyst and purveyor of its will and drives.

At the same time, Nietzsche was well aware that this state "is also a disease that can destroy man," and that "it is still a long way from this morbid isolation, from the desert of these experimental years, to that enormous, overflowing certainty and health which cannot do without illness itself, as an instrument and fishhook of knowledge." Many years of convalescence are needed. Along the way, the free spirit experiences a renewal and rejuvenation of his surroundings. "Those near and nearest things, how they seem to him transformed! What magical fluff they have acquired in the meantime!" And he is "grateful to his travels, to his severity and self-alienation," for he recognizes now that "all pessimism...is thoroughly *cured* by falling ill in the way these free spirits do, staying ill for a good while, and then, for even longer, becoming healthy—I mean 'healthier'."

The themes presented in this preface, of the free spirit's progression through the sickness of suspicion to the health of certainty, of the *necessity* of sickness for health, are further developed in the preface for the second edition of *The Gay Science.* Written approximately six months after that of *Human, All-too-human,* the preface opens with the frank expression of "the gratitude of a convalescent." The entire book, we are told, is

> nothing but a bit of merry-making after long privation and powerlessness, the rejoicing of strength that is returning, of a reawakened faith in a tomorrow and the day after tomorrow, of a sudden sense and anticipation of a future, of impending adventures, of seas that are open again, of goals that are permitted again, believed again.

If we take Nietzsche's words at face value, he was celebrating the escape from a feeling of purposelessness, futility, of a loss of faith—precisely the ways in which he elsewhere describes nihilism.

Nietzsche linked this "stretch of desert, exhaustion, disbelief" to the "determined self-limitation to what was bitter, harsh, and hurtful to know," the consequence of an unrestricted will to truth. But despite the pain of its isolation, Nietzsche said of such sickness, "are we not almost tempted to ask whether we could get along without it?" Why is this sickness so important? Because "only great pain...compels us philosophers to descend into our ultimate depths and to put aside all trust...everything that would interpose a veil." The philosopher—the free spirit of *Human, All-too-human*—deliberately isolates himself from others and seeks to uncover what is hidden, to plumb the depths, to discover truth, marked as he is above all else by "the *will* henceforth to question further, more deeply, severely, harshly, evilly, and quietly than one has questioned heretofore."

Such questioning, however, is a temporary state: "From such abysses, from such severe sickness, also from the sickness of severe suspicion, one returns *newborn*." One acquires a "more delicate taste for joy," and finds within it "a second dangerous innocence." Thus we see here confirmation that Nietzsche regarded nihilism as a potentially restorative and redemptive event, something not only useful, but necessary for the renewed experience of the world.

The prefaces, in other words, coupled with the discussion found in his notebooks, demonstrate that for Nietzsche the advent of nihilism (expressed in the claim, "There is no truth," which leads in turn to the claim, "Nothing has meaning") was necessary, in light of both the way in which we have pursued truth and, more important, the kind of truth we were seeking. Yet its temporary duration was just as necessary as its arrival, given the interpretive character of human existence. Either European culture would perish, under the nothingness that ensues from the death of God and the self-dissolution of Christianity, or the experience of the empty, mendacious character of Platonic-Christian metaphysics would purge it of a way of viewing the world that was both debilitating and false, thereby opening the way for healthier forms of self-expression.

What these forms of self-expression would be, however, is not clear. In part this vagueness stems from Nietzsche's call for individuals to be self-creating, to be free spirits, to be "self-propelled wheels"[25]—far be it from him to predict, much less legislate, the content of post-nihilistic visions of the world. But it also stems from the highly poetic portrayal one such vision receives in *Thus Spoke Zarathustra*. Described by Nietzsche as "the greatest present that has ever been made to [mankind] so far,"[26] *Zarathustra* recounts the experiences and advice of one such transformed individual. Yet the metaphoric, highly literary nature of this work (much more so than Nietzsche's other writings) makes philosophic analysis of it difficult and obscures its meaning.[27]

Despite this vagueness, we may safely state that post-nihilistic interpretations of the world are marked by two related yet possibly contradictory traits. First, they are life-affirming. Unlike nihilistic views (such as Buddhism and Christianity, which deny the reality and truth of the world in which we live, deeming it merely an apparent world, an illusion), post-nihilistic views affirm and value the world in which we live as it is, without recourse to some beyond, some ideal world to give it meaning and value.[28] Linked to this, albeit paradoxically, is the second trait: to affirm life, in some sense means to live as an artist, to create the world anew as one affirms how it already is. Art is understood not as mimetic representation of an external object but as joyous participation in the multiplicity and panoply of existence. The artist, in Nietzsche's eyes, does not judge the world, but exults in it. In other words, one both accepts and transforms the world in which one lives. This would not be possible, however, had one not first passed through and recovered from the "illness" of nihilism, for it is in convalescing from the suspicion of all truth that one experiences the world reborn.

Whatever way one understands this view of life after nihilism, it is important to realize that Nietzsche did not espouse nihilism as an ultimate perspective. Throughout his work one finds a constant commitment to truth which makes his analysis of nihilism possible. Were he not committed to some notion of truth he would not—indeed he could not—argue that nihilism is transitional, nor could he view it as an illness, albeit of a potentially life-enhancing kind.[29]

Precisely because Nietzsche viewed nihilism as a respite, a temporary lull in the search for truth, he was able to argue that it could serve to purge people of false and debilitating world views, potentially leaving them healthier than they were before. His constant appeal to health and sickness, strength and weakness, as criteria for describing interpretive schemes—and for evaluating nihilism—shows that Nietzsche did believe that there existed some reliable and illuminative standard by which to appraise competing world views. Consequently, despite his cynical denunciations of the age in which he lived and his frequently pessimistic prophecies for the future, he maintained his hope and belief in a transfigured world and the possibility of new religious visions. Far from indicating the demise of the religious life, nihilism could, Nietzsche thought, rejuvenate and replenish it. "The free spirit," he wrote, is "the most religious man that there now is" (KSA 10:1 [74]). That he believed the time was ripe for such creation was clear: roughly six months before his collapse, Nietzsche wrote, "And how many new Gods are now possible!... To say it again, how many new Gods are now possible!" (KSA 13:17 [4]).

4

Karl Barth and the Theology of Crisis

THE THEOLOGICAL CONTEXT OF *DER ROEMERBRIEF*

The same year that death finally released Nietzsche from the madness that had imprisoned him for over a decade, Adolf von Harnack, one of the foremost theologians of his day, published a lecture series he had delivered at the University of Berlin entitled *Das Wesen des Christentums.* Described by their author as "a short and plain statement of the Gospel and its history,"[1] these lectures capture the underlying ethos of the tradition known today as Protestant liberalism (or sometimes, usually pejoratively, as "*Kulturprotestantismus*"). The theologians dominating Germany's faculties at the turn of the century did not, in their own eyes, comprise a unified front; but most of the thinkers described as liberals nonetheless shared a common understanding of the nature and task of theological inquiry.[2] If their conclusions differed, they still agreed about the object of investigation: the religious consciousness of Jesus and his followers—and its method: a combination of historical research and psychological introspection.

Harnack's lectures contain in summary form many of the defining traits of liberal theology. The whole gospel, wrote Harnack, is expressed "in the combination of these ideas—God the Father, Providence, the position of men as God's children, [and] the infinite value of the human soul" (68). Focusing on Jesus' message (discovered through critical research on the New Testament intended to cull the kernel of truth from its historical husk), rather than on the crucified and risen Christ, Harnack found the essence of Christianity to lie in its conjoining of religion and morality into one, in the union Jesus created of love and humility. "Religion," Harnack claimed, "may be called the soul of morality, and morality the body of religion" (73), the Kingdom of God being "nothing but the treasure which the soul possesses in the eternal and merciful God" (77). Jesus' divinity, understood by Harnack as "the consciousness which he possessed of being the Son of God," is taken to mean "nothing but the knowledge of God" (128). Rejecting any understanding of the Gospel as containing either a speculative system of thought or a supernaturally revealed truth, Harnack concluded that the Gospel is "a glad message assuring us of life eternal," a message that "teaches us how to live our lives right" and "gives the assurance that, in spite of every struggle, peace, certainty, and something within that can never be destroyed will be the crown of a life rightly led" (146–7).[3]

The optimistic confidence of Harnack's view is a far cry from the nihilistic dissolution prophesied by Nietzsche two decades earlier, and it can therefore be no surprise that Nietzsche's work was largely ignored in theological circles.[4] Far from being in a state of decline, Protestant Christianity seemed to have a power and a breadth unsurpassed in its history, for the Christian community had become, in many eyes, coextensive with the bourgeois liberalism of the day.[5] Not only had Protestantism survived the two major challenges that had confronted it in the nineteenth century—the rise of New Testament criticism and the development of evolutionary theory—but liberal theologians had managed to transform the potentially crippling insights of each into the basis for a modernized version of Christianity. Theology appeared, at the time Harnack was giving his lectures, almost invincible.

Twenty-two years later, with the appearance of the second edition of Barth's *Roemerbrief,* the world in which liberalism had seemed so plausible was gone, having been destroyed in the trenches of the First World War. Barth's commentary served to explode the tottering remains of Protestant liberalism, calling for a radical reorientation of theological inquiry. While not explicitly responding to Harnack's lectures,[6] the book was in fact a programmatic rejection of every one of Harnack's points. Faith is no possession, rather it is a void; God is nowhere present in history, rather the truth points us only to his total absence; Jesus' message lay not in his superior knowledge of God, but in his cry, "My God, My God, why have you forsaken me?" (97) In short, religion "possesses no solution to the problem of life.... What it does is to disclose the truth that [the problem] cannot be solved" (258).[7]

It is tempting to read Barth's commentary as an understandable if extreme reaction to what he elsewhere called "the reeling, rocking, and ruin of culture,"[8] and indeed there was a strongly reactive element to his critique. Barth himself worried about the degree to which his early thought was linked to the post-war mentality as early as 1926, when he asked in the preface to the fourth edition if, rather than interpreting Paul, all he had done was "put into words what was everywhere in the air—especially in Germany after the war?" (23), a question he answered affirmatively in the 1928 preface to the sixth edition: "A great deal of the scaffolding of the book was due to my particular situation at the time, and also to the general situation" (25).[9] To overemphasize this point, however, is to run the risk of overlooking that Barth's "defection" from liberal theology was, in large part, a consequence of his frustrated and failed attempts to make sense out of the theology he had been taught, to make it be what theology, by definition is: the science of God. Alister McGrath correctly notes that "the 'theology of crisis'...developed *within*, rather than *as a result of*, the cultural situation of the post-war period."[10] Barth, perhaps more than some of the others in his circle, had taken liberal theology seriously; it was precisely this seriousness that led him, in 1922, to utter a decisive and unequivocal "NO!" to its method and teaching.

One sees here a small-scale illustration of Nietzsche's claim about the self-dissolving nature of the Christian world view. The liberal theologians taught that we did have access to God, that there was a divine element in our being that, properly cultivated, would flower into a harmonious and beneficent relationship with God. Barth had been educated as a theological liberal; his acceptance of its basic outlook is the most obvious characteristic of his earliest works. Barth began his career, as James D. Smart remarks, a "convinced liberal theologian who, although...in disagreement with some tendencies of liberal scholarship, saw no visible alternative on the horizon."[11] Even as late as 1916 in an address entitled "The Righteousness of God," Barth lauded the human conscience as "the perfect interpreter of life."[12] "We must let conscience speak," Barth wrote, "for it tells of the righteousness of God in such a way that righteousness becomes a certainty." A *certainty*: "What it tells us is no question, no riddle, no problem, but a fact" (10). To respond to this with "humility" and "joy" is faith, a faith that "lets God speak within us" (25).

Yet a scant five years later Barth asserted that "the power of God can be detected neither in the world of nature nor in the souls of men" (*Romans*, 36), that "the insecurity of our whole existence, the vanity and utter questionableness of all that is and of what we are, lies as in a textbook open before us" (46), that mankind is "under judgment...[in] a condition of shattering confusion—from which he can never escape" (85). Barth's position moved, in other words, from a conviction that we do have some means of apprehending God, some experience of the divine, of what is ultimately real, to the conviction that any such claim was illusory, that the only thing that can be said of God is that "God is he whom we do not know" (45). What had happened?

Within Barth's biography one can point to two circumstances which brought home to him the difficulties with a sustained application of Protestant liberalism. First was the appearance of the notorious "Appeal to the World of Culture" in 1914.[13] A document which disavowed any German responsibility for entrance into the war, twelve theologians—including Barth's beloved teacher Wilhelm Herrmann—had signed it, thereby indicating their agreement and support. Barth later wrote,

> One day in early August 1914 stands out in my personal memory as a black day. Ninety-three German intellectuals impressed public opinion by their proclamation in support of the war policy of Wilhelm II and his counselors. Among these intellectuals I discovered to my horror almost all of my theological teachers whom I had greatly venerated. In despair over what this indicated about the signs of the time I suddenly realized that I could no longer follow either their ethics and dogmatics or their understanding of the Bible and of history. For me at least, nineteenth-century theology no longer held any future.[14]

While one might question some of the specifics of Barth's hindsight—"almost all" of his teachers did not sign, nor do his writings start to reflect his rejection of liberalism until almost four years after that date, at the earliest—it must have stirred up suspicions in Barth's mind about the inadequacy, even the danger of liberal theology and its identification of Christianity and culture. If God is believed to be present in history, if divine providence is at work in its events, it is difficult to find theological means to criticize any particular historical occurrence. What happens is in fact the reverse: Christianity is pressed into service as a legitimator of the political and economic situation of the day, something seen in Germany in the early twentieth century in the transformation of *Kulturprotestantismus* into *Kriegstheologie.*[15] Such transformation starkly illustrates the dangers of identifying providence with human history, and in Barth's eyes pointed to the need both to distinguish God from history and to recognize the absolute sovereignty of the word of God and only the word of God.[16]

More important than this particular and isolated event, however, were the continual and insistent demands placed on Barth by his job as a parson at Safenwil. In a letter to Thurneysen, dated November 11, 1918, Barth wrote,

> Just up from the grippe. We must quickly regain our balance in these extraordinary times. But in order to say *what* to ourselves? One stands astonished, doesn't he, and can only state how the face of the world transforms itself, on *this* side of things.... Who is now able to meet things head on, and speak, and act? I was thankful not to have to preach yesterday, and I shudder at the thought of next Sunday.[17]

Barth was not alone in his feelings of confusion and helplessness, and it can be no accident that the other two members of the inner circle of dialectical theology were also struggling with the responsibilities of a pastorate.[18] In the period between the first and the second editions of Barth's commentary,[19] a number of short pieces were written that foreshadow the curious dialectic between nihilism and faith one finds fully laid out in *Der Roemerbrief.* In 1920 Barth's friend Thurneysen published a brief study of Dostoyevsky, offering a theological interpretation of his works.[20] Dostoyevsky is portrayed as raising the question, "What is man?," and as pointing out there is no solution other than "a great dissolution" (14). "Because men have become clever, righteous, wise, and pious *without* God," Thurneysen wrote, "God stands in a corner of the earth and is seen and understood only by those who have been cast out and disinherited, by those who are depraved and corrupt" (47). With a turn of phrase subsequently adopted by Barth, Thurneysen wrote,

> Dostoyevsky does not have any final answer or solution to give to us. His solution is found in the great dissolution;

> his answer is a question, the one burning question of the being of man. But any one who takes up this question will experience that even this question is full of answers. (14)
>
> Precisely because [the solution] is in *God*, and *only* in him, the final word of true knowledge of life can therefore be nothing else than the question about him. Where this question is raised most vigorously, there the meaning of life becomes apparent in its greatest clarity. (44)

Barth's debt to Thurneysen in the reformulation of his position between the first (1919) and second (1922) edition of *Der Roemerbrief* was great, as Barth himself acknowledged. Their correspondence in 1920 reveals that Barth sent Thurneysen each section as it was rewritten for his comments and suggestions. Barth noted in his preface to the second edition that he "adopted [Thurneysen's] additions for the most part without alteration." "So close had been our cooperation," he continued, "that I doubt whether even the specialist could detect where the one leaves off and the other begins" (15).

Nor were Barth and Thurneysen alone in their outlook. This same year Friedrich Gogarten published a short but explosive essay entitled *"Zwischen den Zeiten"* (literally, "Between the Times") in *Die christliche Welt*, the chief organ of liberal theology. In a fervent tone characterized by a curious mixture of self-righteousness and despair, Gogarten, speaking for the younger generation, rejected the speech of his elders as "hollow" and "empty," in which nothing could be heard "but the best intentions." The liberal focus on culture and history as the means of approaching the divine had resulted in the condition, according to Gogarten, that, "We are so deeply immersed in humanity that we have lost God. Lost him. Yes, really lost him. None of our thoughts reach beyond the human sphere. Not a single one."[21] Gogarten closed his essay by raising the question "in all seriousness whether today there are any men who can really conceive of God" (282).

One might conclude from *"Zwischen den Zeiten"* that the hopelessness of the present situation led Gogarten to despair of any possible theological response to it, yet in an essay published a few months later, it is clear that despair is only part of the picture. It is necessary, Gogarten wrote, "to pass through the deepest skepticism, the darkest pessimism" before genuine faith can find expression, a faith which "one cannot *have*" but which "one can only practice."[22] "Any objective certainty is out of the question for the religious way of thinking" (290), for true religion is identical with the "crisis of culture," the judgment upon and dissolution of every possible human content or possession. "God has no place in a world until man first utterly annihilates himself" (290), for "in this state of utter debasement—and only here—can the divine values arise; and only in this state of meaninglessness can the eternal meaning of all things shine through" (295). Like Thurneysen, Gogarten believed that religious meaning was accessible only through confrontation with a radical and despairing meaninglessness.

After reading Gogarten's essay and meeting with him, Barth wrote to Thurneysen,

> Here is a dreadnought on our side and against our opponents. Who knows, perhaps one day he will teach us something! He has quite the manners and also the equipment to be the very man who...I have great expectations concerning him. At any rate he will provide some very uncomfortable times for the CW [*Die christliche Welt*] folk and perhaps one day he will make some kind of enormous breach in the theological wall. Apparently there is a trickle beginning already.[23] (Barth's ellipsis)

Little did Barth know that it was he, and not Gogarten who would prove to be the "dreadnought," and one who would be responsible for not merely a breach, but the collapse of Protestant liberalism.

The significance of Barth's revised commentary on Romans does not lie in being the earliest expression of the fundamental ambiguity of faith—for, as we have seen, at least two of Barth's colleagues claim that the "answer" of faith is to be found only in the radical questionableness of all things—but in being the first sustained attempt to ground this understanding of Christianity in the New Testament. And despite the fact that it became—some said by his intent—the manifesto of dialectical theology, Barth did not regard himself as presenting a radically new theology, a new "ism," or a theory of religion disguised as scriptural commentary. Rather, as he stated unequivocally in the preface to the English translation in 1933, his "sole aim was to interpret scripture." Consequently, he thought that the only question that should be brought to the book is, "Did Paul speak in general and in detail in the manner in which I [Barth] have interpreted him as thinking and speaking? Or did he think and speak altogether differently?" (ix-x). The author would have us approach the book, in other words, solely in terms of the accuracy and faithfulness of its interpretation of Paul's interpretation of the Christ event.

For this reason, if no other, the unprecedented response, both for and against, provoked by the appearance of the second edition in 1922 caused Barth considerable pause, even consternation, in hindsight.[24] The reviews to the first edition had been sufficiently favorable to win him a chair in theology at Goettingen, no small feat for a pastor from Switzerland. Yet precisely the approval of these reviews caused Barth "such dismay" that he decided when his publisher requested a second edition that he "had sometimes to express the matter otherwise, sometimes even to adopt an entirely different position" (4), with the result that the book was completely rewritten. Barth's use of contentiousness as a hermeneutical principle, however, backfired, if we take his words at face value, and the proliferation of Barthians in the wake of the second and third editions made him uneasy.

By 1924, Barth felt that book "obviously" needed further revision, but he had neither the time nor the energy for its undertaking. In 1926 he stated, almost petulantly, "I often wish that I had never written it," stating that "it has gained the applause by which it is condemned" (22–3). By 1932, with the preface to the English translation, he was "begging" his readers to take the book "solely on its own merits," independent of any preconceptions about "Barthianism" or "Dialectical Theology," commenting, "when I look back at the book, it seems to have been written by another man to meet a situation belonging to a past epoch" (vi).

In light of the subsequent course of Barth's thought, his growing disenchantment with *Der Roemerbrief* can easily be seen as a reflection of his increasing orientation around a purely God-centered theology (sometimes referred to as a "positivism of revelation"). The problem was less with the words in *Der Roemerbrief* themselves—Barth later remarked that while not in themselves wrong, each statement needed to be tempered with a corresponding opposite statement to correct the infectious influence of Kierkegaard and existentialism[25]—than the impact they had and the kind of negative natural theology that ensued from them.

Despite Barth's repeated insistence that he was not interested in founding a new theological school, his voice rang like that of an Old Testament prophet across the war-ravaged terrain of Germany. The power of Barth's rhetoric, coupled with the timeliness of the commentary's appearance, prompted a positive response primarily among younger theologians, theologians who had, like Barth, been trained in Protestant liberalism, and, also like Barth, found its promise counterfeit. *Der Roemerbrief* rejuvenated ministers who found preaching difficult, if not impossible, under the old rhetoric. Paul Tillich, commenting on the work, wrote that "the extraordinary effect that Barth's book is having is summed up in the words of one pastor: 'it is now possible to preach again!'"[26]

Together with Thurneysen and Gogarten, Barth founded a journal whose name was taken from Gogarten's essay: "*Zwischen den Zeiten.*"[27] The title captures the estranged and apocalyptic sensibility that informed the work of these theologians, much as *Die christliche Welt* expressed the self-understanding of their liberal forebears. The journal—like dialectical theology itself—was relatively shortlived. Dissolved in 1933 by significant ideological differences between its members,[28] one nevertheless finds the spirit and characteristic insight operative in Barth's theology of crisis influential into the 1950s in the work of Bultmann, Reinhold Niebuhr, and Paul Tillich, in the 1960s and 70s in the death-of-God theology of Altizer and Robinson, and even in the 1980s in the deconstructive theology of Mark C. Taylor and Charles Raschke.[29]

Two fundamental premises drive Barth's argument forward: first, that people long for security, foundation, and assurance; second, that no such foundation or assurance is to be had in this life. Put theologically, Barth's view is underwritten by the belief that people crave God but that God is absent in the world. In a brilliant, if ultimately self-defeating, move Barth managed to construct from these two premises a soteriology of ambiguity, characterized by the insistence that "in the radical dissolution of all physical, intellectual, and spiritual achievements of men, in the all-embracing 'relativization' of all human distinctions and human dignities, their true and eternal meaning is made known" (78). The move is brilliant, for it transforms the advent of Nietzsche's "uncanniest of all guests" into a religiously charged event; self-defeating, for, as we shall see, the legitimation of nihilism inevitably drains it of its transformative power.

Barth's method in this work—and throughout his early theology—is "dialectical," which means that it operates by means of the juxtaposition of opposites, not in order to sublate both in a higher unity, but to call attention to the dizzying tension between the two, and to affirm the reality of both in face of the impossibility yet the truth of their conjunction. In the abyss created by their juxtaposition lies the sole truth accessible to human existence. Paradox, yes. But not, as one unsympathetic critic put it, "because the sacrifice of the intellect is a pleasure for those who here have little to sacrifice,"[30] rather, because only through the confrontation with genuine paradox is one stripped free of one's pretensions to know—and thereby stripped of one's illusions. One is forced to confront what one is—and is not—in a direct, unmediated fashion. Despite his constant indictments of the nineteenth-century cult of religious experience, Barth's early thought is itself through and through an attempt to cultivate a certain kind of experience—of the radical annihilation of every human possibility and confidence, or, as we have put it above, existential or axiological nihilism—to bring people face to face with who they are.[31]

Because Barth believed that his point could only be communicated "dialectically" rather than "dogmatically" or "critically,"[32] a set of problems confronts the expositor of Barth similar to that confronting the expositor of Kierkegaard's pseudonymous authorship: how to communicate non-dialectically, that is, directly, what the author believed could only be communicated dialectically, indirectly? The similarity to Kierkegaard is no accident, since Barth's early allegiance to Kierkegaard is as certain as his subsequent repudiation of him.[33] Fortunately, my attempt in this work is scholarly rather than apologetic or therapeutic. My goal is not to cultivate the experience in my readers that Barth was appealing to, but rather to characterize this experience as presented in *Der Roemerbrief,* to describe how we are to understand the logic undergirding this apologetic appropriation of nihilism, and, finally, to discuss whether we can make sense of the conditions that make such a move possible.

A SOTERIOLOGY OF AMBIGUITY

The position Barth laid out in *Der Roemerbrief* is best understood within the context of its radically dualistic metaphysics, inherited from Kierkegaard, on the one hand, and Kant and Plato, on the other. This dualism is both the most obvious feature of the work and the means whereby Barth condemned liberalism's theological paradigm as fallacious. It was also the driving force behind his advocacy of a view of faith so radically contentless that it is theoretically indistinguishable from nihilism.

In the preface to the second edition, Barth wrote:

> If I have a system, it is limited to a recognition of what Kierkegaard called the "infinite qualitative distinction" between time and eternity, and to my regarding this as possessing negative as well as positive significance: "God is in his heaven, and thou art on earth." (10)

At that time only recently translated into German,[34] Kierkegaard is today well-known for his rejection of both the state church of Denmark (a politically sanctioned form of culture protestantism) and the ameliorative philosophy of speculative idealism prevalent during the first half of the nineteenth century. In opposition to the grand synthesis of absolute *Geist* posited by Hegel (and eagerly accepted by his followers, self-styled "epigones") Kierkegaard's thought stressed paradox, disjunction, and the presence of basic ruptures in existence. Life is not one great whole, in Kierkegaard's eyes, in which all contradiction is eventually sublated in the unity of *Geist*'s perfect self-consciousness, but a sequence of breaks and fissures that can be held together, if at all, solely through the "passionate inwardness" of an individual.[35]

Barth's acceptance of Kierkegaard's "infinite qualitative distinction" between time and eternity, between God and man, was reinforced by the Platonic/Kantian distinction between the true and the apparent world, between the world as it really is (the noumenal realm) and the world given to us through human perception (the phenomenal realm).[36] Barth accepted the Kantian dictum that our knowledge is limited to the world of appearance, to the historical, changing sphere in which we live; of its ground or its source we can in principle know nothing. To Barth this meant that all of our knowledge is limited to the human realm: of God we can know nothing, except that, "He is whom we do not know" (*Romans*, 45).

Barth used this radical dualism to support his conviction that liberal theology had been guilty of the most serious error possible: the confounding of God and man, the ontological confusion of the human and the divine realms. The consequence of such a confusion is the total loss of God:

> Thinking of ourselves what can be thought of God, we are unable to think of him more highly than we think of ourselves. Being to ourselves what God ought to be to us, he is no more to us than we are to ourselves. This secret identification of ourselves with God carries with it our own isolation from him. (45)

We misunderstand who God is, and also who we are, and therefore live in a great and profound illusion, alienated both from God and from ourselves.

Protestant liberalism itself was informed by the Kantian critique of reason and metaphysics, but drew quite different conclusions from it. For the liberal theologians, its acceptance pointed to the necessity for reflection upon the experience of faith and its conditions of possibility. Following a program first set by Schleiermacher, theology was thought to consist of articulating the characteristics of the faithful consciousness, for it is in this way—through the examination of the faithful subject—that the image of the object can be discovered.[37] The Kantian strategy was further combined with the evolutionary historicism of Hegelianism, which inevitably softened the sharp distinction drawn by Kant between the noumenal and the phenomenal world, making the difference more a matter of degree than of kind. Consequently, the liberals portrayed Jesus as a superior human being, marked by a knowledge of God which other humans empirically lacked but which they could theoretically, and would eventually, attain.

Barth's dualism was, in contrast, sharp and absolute, stressing the qualitative, even the ontological, difference between the two. This change in large part can be attributed to a growing awareness of the double-edged nature of historical inquiry and of the meaning of historicity. It was still widely held in the nineteenth century that through historical investigation and reflection one could gain knowledge of the absolute, the eternal. But by the twentieth century, the split between the phenomenal and the noumenal world had grown to encompass the split between the historical and the particular, on the one side, and the absolute and the universal, on the other. The radical historicism of Ernst Troeltsch, for example, taught that historicity means relativity, and that relativity means ambiguity.[38]

Troeltsch still hoped for the possibility of attaining religious knowledge in some form, but for Barth and many of his contemporaries, the philosophical and theological difficulties of historicism were completely overshadowed by the existential refutation of historical pantheism by World War I. For Barth the issue was no longer how we can best ground theology in historical reflection, but, how do we even make sense out of the inchoate mess that is our existence? How can we claim to know anything about God at all, when "what is clearly seen to be indisputable reality is the invisibility of God"? (46). God is so far removed from our experience that one is even driven to question his very existence.

> [Our] world is formless and tumultuous chaos, a chaos of the forces of nature and of the human soul. [Our] life is illusion. This is the situation in which we find ourselves. The question, "Is there then a God?" is therefore entirely relevant and indeed inevitable. (37)

Barth epitomized in 1921 Nietzsche's portrayal of the person who discovers that the true world which he or she had been promised, the God of the liberals, is but an illusion and a sham. All we have around us is a world of "formless and tumultuous chaos," no longer supported by the ground and foundation which gave it its meaning.

Since the liberal response to Kantian dualism would no longer work—and was, in fact, part of the problem—Barth had to try another tack. Given his insistence on the absolute distinction between God and man, between the human and divine realm, any intermingling of the two would be a logical impossibility—in Kierkegaard's words, a paradox. God is in his heaven, and we are on earth, and the two are absolutely incommensurable. Any contact between the two is, from our point of view—indeed, from any point of view we could possibly hold—impossible. Human distance from God (classically speaking, "sin") is so great that any rejoining of the two ("salvation," which brings righteousness) is impossible. Yet one finds in the New Testament the good news that God has become man, that humans are made righteous despite their sin, that salvation is theirs, although unmerited and undeserved. One finds witness to the existence and reality of faith, despite its impossibility, and the gracious love of God, despite its invisibility.

One way to think of Barth's approach to what he termed the "impossible possibility of faith" is as a curious version of Kant's move in *The Critique of Pure Reason*. Grant that there is faith; how is this possible? Barth's problem, in other words, was to describe the impossible possibility of faith in terms that would be true to both the ontological separation of God and man and the widespread experience of the absence of God and the meaninglessness and futility of all human endeavors. How to reconcile a God who loves with the contrasting apparent annihilation and devaluation of everything human? How to make sense even out of God's existence, in light of his marked absence from the world?[39]

Barth's solution was to lay out a view of the world and an interpretation of Paul which ties faith to the experience of meaninglessness and futility. The annihilation of human possibility becomes God's judgment upon man; his absence from the world, a consequence of human sin; the presence of faith despite its impossibility, the effect of his gracious love. To convey this without turning faith into a human possession—without thereby undermining his polemic against the liberals—Barth had to speak continually in paradox, i.e., dialectically. Faith is completely empty, devoid of any possible content, predicated upon the shattering of all human claims to know the true and the good.

It was precisely Barth's radical dualism, his conviction that God is, in the words of Rudolf Otto, "wholly other," that enabled him to make this connection between faith and nihilism.[40] His postulation that God is nowhere to be found in the world enabled him to describe grace as a total transformation of the individual. Because the transformation is total, it must be perceived as negation:

> The word of God is the transformation of everything that we know as Humanity, Nature, and History, and must therefore be apprehended as the negation of the starting point of every system of which we are capable of conceiving. (278)

Because of the complete rupture between the divine and the human, because "the 'Something' that the word of God creates is of an eternal order, wholly distinct from every 'something' that we know otherwise," we cannot but view the working of God as the denial and the rejection of everything we know and can imagine: "Compared with our 'something' it is and remains always—nothing" (102). The effect of grace, in other words, is the complete annihilation of all confidence, of every security—existential, epistemic, and moral—that previously defined our lives. "Restless and terribly shattering, grace completely overthrows the foundations of this world" (103). The new person that we are to become, therefore, "emerges in the negation of the old, known, human subject" (150). And it is only through this negation that grace—divine love—is realized.

As a consequence of this—and in anticipation of the deconstructive attack on traditional value hierarchies—traditional relationships become inverted. Religion becomes unbelief, because religion claims to possess knowledge of God which, given God's absolute unknowability, is impossible. Religion is a cultural, i.e., a human, product, and therefore stands under the same indictment as every other human thing. The atheist, who denies the existence of God, is closer to the truth than the traditional theist, who affirms a God who can only be understood as an extension of the world. "Indeed, a certain perception is betrayed when we begin to reject the no-God of unbelief" (43), that is, when we abandon belief in the God upheld by conventional religion. The atheist and the critic of religion are to be commended for their recognition of the idolatrous nature of religious belief (which claims to worship God, but in truth only worships human beings), and for having the "courage of despair" that must ensue, in Barth's eyes, from blatant atheism (40).

The dismantling of false beliefs, motivated by "a grim horror of illusion...by a genuine refusal to be deceived by those penultimate and antepenultimate truths with which human research has to be content" (87) is, for Barth, "the road to negation," a road which is simultaneously "the road to the eternal meaning of the created world," the only road possible. Barth wrote,

> What is pleasing to God comes into being when all human righteousness is gone, irretrievably gone, when men are uncertain and lost, when they have abandoned all ethical and religious illusions, and when they have renounced every hope in this world and in this heaven. (68)

For Barth, it is "in the midst of the last and deepest skepticism that there may perhaps exist that brokenness which is the recollection of God, aye, of God himself" (67). God "must not be sought as though he sat enthroned upon the summit of religious attainment. He is to be found on the plain where men suffer and sin" (132). "The veritable pinnacle of religious achievement," in other words, "is attained when men are thrust into the company of those who lie in the depths" (132).

Consequently, the task of an apostle is always "purely negative": In an apostle "a void becomes visible" (33). A void, because God is not something in the world which we can see. God can be experienced in this world only as emptiness, only as nothingness, only as denial, rejection, abandonment. "God," wrote Barth, "is pure negation" (141). Even Christ's achievement, Barth argued,

> is a negative achievement. He is not a genius, endowed with manifest or even with occult powers; he is not a hero or leader of men; he is neither poet nor thinker:—*My God, My God, why hast thou forsaken me?* (97)

Christ's "achievement," in other words, is his abandonment by God in face of his devotion. Jesus is the Christ because

> he sacrifices to the incomparably greater and to the invisibly other every claim to genius and every human heroic or aesthetic or psychic possibility, because there is no conceivable human possibility of which he did not rid himself. (97)

Precisely this annihilation and dissolution of all human possibility is, for Barth, the premise of faith, for "the divine answer is given only in the veritably final and veritably insoluble human problem" (258). Consequently, the sole thing that either religion or ethics—human attempts to realize the divine and the good—can do is to bring the individual face to face with the inadequacy of thought and the impotence of action, with the fundamental brokenness of human existence. "The function of Christianity, its achievement, is to bring [the relativity of every concrete action] to our notice. The absolute character of Christian ethics lies in the fact that they are altogether problematical" (465). For this reason, the Gospel is "not a truth among other truths," but rather the setting of a "great question mark against all other truths" (35). The sole achievement of religion is the shattering of every self-certainty. "Religion is the place where, in the world of time and of things and of men, the intolerable question is clearly formulated—who, then, art thou?" (268). The questionableness of my own existence is forced upon me by the basic rupture in my being, revealed to me by the ethical demand. "I do not practice what is good, I perform all manner of evil that I would not. And so the question arises once again: who, then, am I?" (265). "The reality of religion...lies precisely in the questionableness of my **ego**" (266).

Barth's position thus far is that genuine faith, the expression of true religious being, is essentially linked to the dissolution of all human possibility, to the confrontation with the emptiness of the world and the questionable, ambiguous nature of every human thought and action. Faith appears, in other words, to be inextricably bound up with, even identical to, the nihilism that Nietzsche saw as predicated upon the dissolution of Christianity. To use the more technical vocabulary introduced in Chapter Two, Barth embraces as central to faith the existential, moral, and epistemological nihilism that ensues from the self-destruction of liberal protestantism. Does this mean, therefore, that nothing differentiates the genuine religious believer, as Barth portrayed this person, from the despairing atheist? What, if anything, distinguishes faith from nihilism, on this model?

Because Barth's radical dualism of the divine and the human realm is mirrored in the sharp distinction he drew between the "old man" prior to faith and the "new man" transformed by faith, there is a temptation to read Barth as though he were saying that faith appears to be nihilism only to those who don't participate in it. "To unbelief, [God's] righteousness is necessarily manifested as divine negation" (93). Once faith is made real, however, the situation changes. Through the spectacles of faith, the believer "see[s] the invisible. [He or she sees] the righteousness of God in his wrath, the risen Christ in the crucified one, life in death, the 'Yes' in the 'No'" (156). Such statements suggest that once grace has acted, once the transformation of the individual from the old to the new man has taken place, the world appears quite differently. The experience of nihilism, in other words, would be a kind of spiritual cleansing, readying the individual for the infusion of grace, but subsequently superseded by the calm assurance of one who has been reborn. What is unknown to the unbeliever—in Barth's terminology, to the "old man," the person standing "on this side" of the resurrection—is both known and intelligible to the believer—the "new man," the person standing "on the other side" of the resurrection.

In comments like this Barth appears to be making the standard religious claim that certain truths are sensible only to people standing within the boundaries of faith: Only those who share the Christian outlook find the tenets of the Christian faith meaningful and intelligible. Once accepted, these beliefs are not only meaningful in themselves, but they serve to make the world meaningful. Nihilistic despair is simply the means whereby we are catapulted into faith, but once having gotten there, so to speak, the world becomes a place of meaning, harmony, and truth.

This reading, however, cannot long be supported. What Gertrude Stein said of Oakland applies equally well to the position of the faithful: "There's no 'there' there." In Barth's words,

> Just as surely as the recognition of the sovereignty of God overthrows all confidence in human righteousness, it sets erect no other ground of confidence. Men are not deprived of one security, in order that they may immediately discover for themselves another. No man can shelter himself behind the triumphant will of God; rather, when it is once perceived, he comes under judgment and enters a condition of shattering confusion—from which he can never escape. (85)

This passage implies that, if anything, the new man is *more* despairing than the atheist; at least, certainly, *as* despairing. Despite the transformation effected in the conversion from the old to the new man, Barth insisted that in the new man, "No union of God and man is consummated," which means that "the bitter conflict between flesh and spirit remains as intense as before" and that "the tension of the paradox remains without even the slightest easement. Men are compelled to wait and only to wait; they are impelled to hope, and not to sight" (151).

Barth was trying to walk a very fine line here. On the one hand, he had to affirm that there is meaning in negation, since, as he put it, negation is "God's way of saving us." If the believer is to be distinguished from the atheist at all, there must be more to life than what the atheist sees. On the other hand, he had to resist all attempts to make faith something secure, a possession held by the believer which, once acquired, cannot be lost, because this would undermine the absolute disjunction he presumed between this world and the divine realm, and make him guilty of the liberal's error. Hence he was left in the somewhat precarious position of asserting the complete contentlessness of faith. He emphasized repeatedly that faith is a void or vacuum (*ein Hohlraum*); it means "motionlessness, silence, worship—it means not-knowing" (202).

Thus, while Barth did at times speak of the believer's "knowledge" that despair and negation are divine tools for human salvation, this "knowledge" bears no resemblance to anything we would customarily describe as such. Faith has, literally, no content, for the believer is in possession of no fact, no datum, that is hidden to the non-believer. The "knowledge" of faith, one might say, is dispositional rather than propositional. Faith bespeaks an attitudinal transformation on the part of the believer, not a cognitive one. Barth wrote,

> Faith is conversion: it is the radically new disposition of the man who stands naked before God and has been wholly impoverished that he may procure the one pearl of great price; it is the attitude of the man who for the sake of Jesus has lost his own soul. (98)

The sole difference, it would appear, between the atheist and the Christian is the simple yet inexplicable fact that while both despair, the Christian nonetheless hopes.

One might object that believers do possess something, or at least, think they do, and that the just quoted passage clearly indicates what this something is: Jesus. And this possession necessarily can be expressed in terms of beliefs held about the world. One might argue that any disposition, any state of mind can be mapped out in terms of a set of propositions accepted and believed true. The Christian's attitude of hopeful supplication, in other words, is simply the emotional concomitant of his or her belief that Jesus is the Christ, and that through him we gain eternal life.

While it is true that Christians might—in fact, do—express their faith in terms of statements affirming the divinity of Christ and the meaning and power of his resurrection, one would be hard pressed to describe these statements as propositions, even as convictions, in any normal linguistic usage. Philosophers of religion have long since sensitized us to the peculiar status of many religious claims; the more hostile critics have argued that statements like "Jesus is the Christ" are, at bottom, meaningless, because they lack any specifiable verifiable content. On this view, to say "Jesus is the Christ" is really to say nothing more than "Jesus" in a trusting tone of voice.

Barth, oddly enough, agreed with this. "The assumption that Jesus is the Christ is, in the strictest sense of the word, an assumption, void of any content that can be comprehended by us" (36). Christ, God, eternity are absolutely unknown and unintelligible to us because they are words that signify the non-historical, the non-temporal, the non-relative. We can fill them with no content that makes them comprehensible, because we can operate only in terms of the historical, the relative, the contingent. Consequently, any statement made about faith or from faith is more than simply paradoxical—identifying two diametrically opposed notions, such as time and eternity—but ultimately devoid of meaning, because it "defines" the intelligible in terms that are in principle unintelligible. Strictly speaking, said Barth, we "cannot believe. We can only believe that we believe" (150).

Is there then no difference between the atheist and the Christian? In the final analysis there is—and indeed there has to be, if Barth's polemic against the liberals was to be coherent. The "infinite qualitative distinction" between God and man was used by Barth to underscore the centrality of grace in the realization of faith and the impossibility of any natural theology (i.e., an attempt to move from the world to God by using reason or reflection.)[41] Consequently, Barth had to distinguish between the atheist and the Christian, between humanly created nihilistic despair and faith, if he was to avoid falling victim to the chief error of theological liberalism: confusing the human and the divine. So, while Barth acknowledged that the atheist was, in one sense, on the right track for rejecting idolatrous forms of religion, he also asserted that no merely human conviction of relativity is sufficient for faith. Barth wrote, "Men are not justified by their perception of so fruitful an insecurity, as though it were a human achievement by which they could be reconciled to God. Not even this apprehension is sufficient to provide them with the longed for certainty" (194-5).

This is more than simply a case of allowing one's polemical needs to determine one's theoretical position. Barth argued, in effect, that human efforts at negation would inevitably fall short of the complete and total upheaval essential for faith.

> No man can of himself utter the humiliating fact that he is—a man.... The man who not only criticizes, disapproves of, and deplores himself, but is able finally to set his whole being in question, is, at any rate, not I. (271)

Merely human negation is not sufficient, for it simply cannot go far enough. As Barth wrote elsewhere, "no self-negation...(were it even suicide!) is so great and so profound as the actuality, as the self-negation to which all other negativities can only point, the self-negation which is immediately imbued with the positivity of God."[42] Total dissolution, in other words, can only come from God.

This restriction of the scope of nihilism is oddly consistent with what many other thinkers have written about nihilism. We saw it earlier, for example, in Nietzsche, both in his portrayal of humans as inevitably interpretive creatures and in his speculation that nihilism "may be a divine way of thinking." Nihilism is for Nietzsche necessarily a temporary condition, since human beings are constitutionally forced to interpret their surroundings. The ability to suspend the interpretive process is, Nietzsche implied, a divine attribute, not a human one. Most thinkers agree that perfect nihilism is a limiting concept, not something that could be humanly realized.[43] To be a perfect nihilist would be to be dead, because the act of living involves some positive judgments about the world, if made only by default. Hence the radical dissolution of all human possibility, the annihilation of all belief, would have to be the effect of grace, a divinely given possibility.[44]

If full-fledged nihilism was, in Barth's eyes, only a possibility if it came from God, we can see then how he could assert that "the divine answer is given only in the veritably final and veritably insoluble human problem" (278). In so far as God "gives" the question, he is also "given" with the question. This enabled Barth to say, therefore, that "the final meaning of our temporal existence lies in our questioning as to its meaning" (437).[45] If this is not the case, "If the last question which faith proposed is not—as the last question—at once the answer to all questions," Barth wrote, "then faith is not faith, and we have concluded wrongly" (116).

Thus part of what distinguishes the atheist from the Christian, nihilism from faith, is that the despair and the uncertainty of the Christian is incomparably greater than that of the atheist. How, then, to explain hope?

Part of the answer lies in the simple statement that hope is the this-worldly expression of God's grace. It is part of the "impossible possibility" that can only be explained at the cost of its own undermining. Explaining the hope of the faithful is like explaining grace—it cannot be done without destroying it. Nonetheless there is within

Barth's remarks an implicit if problematic premise about the nature of hope: that hope necessarily depends upon the absence of its object in order to exist. "We cannot transform hope—and deny it—by making of it a present reality" (53). To hope for an object one has or knows is not real hope. "Not to see, to be deprived and empty-handed, to be confronted by negation—this is what hope means.... To *rejoice in hope* means to know God in hope without seeing him, and to be satisfied that it should be so" (457). Genuine faith, in other words, is only possible within the context of nihilism, for only in this situation is the object of faith missing.

RELIGIOUS NIHILISM

More than one commentator has noted that "all human thought, devotion, and love [are] so strictly excluded from faith that one can almost say that Barth's radical Christianity leads him to atheism."[46] While insightful, in so far as such comments recognize the intimate connection between atheistic nihilism and genuine religious faith in Barth's understanding of Christianity, they obscure a central aspect of this relationship. For Barth, nihilism was not the end result of theological inquiry, but, in an important sense, its point of departure; nor is nihilism presented as an alternative to Christian faith, but as an essential part of its makeup.

Barth did not move from conventional religious belief to nihilism in *Der Roemerbrief*; rather, he began with nihilism, deepening it and giving it a religious interpretation whereby it culminates in faith. Barth believed that *no* human knowledge was possible; we are completely isolated and shut off from God and from truth, and this realization throws us into despair. He was, in other words, an epistemological nihilist—rejecting knowledge as a means to truth—whose recognition of this fact led to existential nihilism. But note that nowhere does Barth abandon his belief in God. The completeness of the despair and the irrefutable reality of God's absence is used as a peculiar form of testimony to God's presence. Full-fledged nihilism, as we have seen, is for Barth a gift of God, bringing with it, paradoxically, a dispositional transposition of human beings that enables them to respond to the emptiness around them with hope and love.

This view is laid out more explicitly by Rudolf Bultmann in his 1924 essay, "Liberal Theology and the Latest Theological Movement,"[47] in which he sets out his interpretation of the Barthian dynamic between faith and nihilism. "*Man's fundamental sin,*" Bultmann wrote, "*is his will to justify himself as man,* for thereby he makes himself God." The will to self-justification is seen in every human attempt to find a ground or foundation for existence.

When one recognizes that this attempt inevitably fails, for all such foundations are merely human projections, human interpretations, and not a genuine ground, "the whole world is taken off its hinges.... The whole world—which was *man's* world—is annihilated; nothing in it any longer has meaning and value, for everything has received this from man." One is forced to recognize the purely human, purely contingent, purely apparent character of all of our claims to possess the truth, to have justified ourselves. This recognition is precisely the judgment of God. "To know this judgment," Bultmann continued, "is also to know it as grace, since it is really liberation. Man becomes free from himself." That is, one is released from one's ties to the purely contingent, basically false world in which one lives; one becomes free. "And for man to become free from himself is redemption" (46-7). To be free from the human world is to open oneself to the possibility of the new creation.

This experience of annihilation is, for Bultmann as it was for Barth, the cause of despair. Yet it is not a despair subsequently supplanted by faith. Bultmann wrote, echoing Barth,

> The despair is not conceived as a sort of overwhelming preliminary stage which must be surmounted so that it

> may be followed by the consciousness of redemption. The despair, radically conceived, is the realization that the natural man is trying to flee from before God and that he cannot flee because he was trying to flee before *God*. That despair, therefore, comes only when there is awareness of God. But when there is awareness of God as God, flight has ended and a turning to God has begun. There are not two acts. (50)

Thus, for Bultmann as well as for Barth, faith has at its core a kind of nihilism.

In his article "The Doctrines of God and Man in the Theology of Rudolf Bultmann,"[48] K. E. Logstrup stressed this same point. The relation to the world found in the Christian faith and in nihilism is the same. In both cases, the world is renounced as a source of meaning and value. And since faith is devoid of any content—a "*das*" with no "*was*"—faith points to no unequivocal new source of meaning. While nihilistic despair is an essential precondition of genuine faith—"there is no other way to an understanding and recognition of the Beyond than through nihilism," for "the question of the Beyond does not arise until the nothingness of the world and of one's own existence has been fully apprehended"—it is not followed by a faith characterized by confident assurance: "Nihilism is not a thing of the past that has been left behind; on the contrary, it has been accepted as an established element of the Christian faith" (84).

Yet does not such a view merely continue the liberal focus on the character of present existence as the expression of divinity? Brian Gerrish aptly comments,

> Some of us may wonder why it was culture-Protestantism to have been optimistic in an age of progress, but *not* culture-Protestantism to have been gloomy in an age of despair. A still later generation...may be inclined to look back impartially on both the liberal action and the neo-orthodox counteraction as formally similar responses to different cultural moods.[49]

A related point is made by Hans Zahrnt:

> By stressing so forcibly God's negation in the midst of the general misery of the time, and virtually snatching his judgment from him, [dialectical theology] runs the risk of surreptitiously making the historical situation, and therefore something within time and within the world, a negative point of contact for God's act of revelation.[50]

Barth and his circle, in other words, have appeared to make a virtue out of the particular historical situation in which they found themselves, a move that parallels what was in their eyes the sin of the liberals. This, in turn, invites the charge that

> the sudden success of [Barth's] *Commentary on Romans* was due to the fact that its fundamental conception of man was the conception of the post-war period. Nothing had to be corrected. It was possible to maintain the common understanding of life, but at the same time [Barth] was able to insert Christ and the New Testament into this framework in a new and novel manner.[51]

Barth did at times make statements calling his time "peculiar," because "in much greater measure than the time just preceding it presents the problem of ethics as a real concern, as a true *problem*."[52] Given his view that the true goal of ethics and religion is to point to their own problematic character, the clear presumption of such remarks is that the present age is in some important sense privileged.

Yet despite the understandable conviction that the times in which they lived were extraordinary, none of these men could have been unaware that a glorification of the present historical situation not only posed major theological problems but also seriously undermined their own position. Barth himself quickly worried about how much his early views were linked to the epoch in which they came to light, as we have seen above. And in different ways, each member of Barth's circle sought to correct this tendency.

Most of the dialectical theologians appealed to some

version of existentialism. The use of an allegedly timeless view of the self neatly avoided the problem of making a particular historical situation special.[53] The link between nihilism and faith was seen as built into the structure of human existence, something, therefore, that would be true not just in Germany in the aftermath of World War I, but in any historical situation. Bultmann in fact argued that Heideggerian categories expressed in philosophic form the same concerns and picture of the world one found in the New Testament, and that therefore they were the most useful tools for biblical exegesis.[54]

Barth, however, chose another route, opting for what Dietrich Bonhoeffer labelled a "positivism of revelation,"[55] making the word of God the sole possible basis and object of theological inquiry. In his eyes, replacing a special historical situation with a particular philosophical view as the key to genuine faith did not avoid the problem of a natural theology at all; it was rather a continued instance of the same move found in all attempts to reason analogically toward God. Already in 1922 he wrote,

> I have heard that crisis is a dialectical conception which not only allows but calls for its opposite—that this negation, which *removes* from human conduct all false values, may *restore* to it new value, may return to it its original value—that the question may be its own *answer* and the argument *against* man be the argument *for* him.[56]

This was a potentially dangerous misinterpretation of the theology of crisis, in his eyes. We must be wary, he said, of "taking refuge in dialectic" (151), adding, "There is no way from us to God—not even a *via negativa*—not even a *via dialectica* nor *paradoxica*. The God who stood at the end of some human way—even of this way—would not be God" (170). Barth wrote to Bultmann in 1930,

> From my standpoint all of you [Bultmann, Gogarten, Brunner, among others]...represent a large scale return to the fleshpots of Egypt. I mean that if I am not deceived, all of you—in a new way different from that of the nineteenth

> century—are trying to understand faith as a human possibility, or if you will, as grounded in a human possibility, and therefore you are once again surrendering theology to philosophy. Where people play around with a natural theology and are so eager to pursue theology within the framework of a preunderstanding that has not been attained theologically, the inevitable result is that they end up in rigidities and reactionary corners which are no better than the liberalisms of others.[57]

This disagreement about the status of natural theology led to the 1933 dissolution of *Zwischen den Zeiten,* with Barth and Thurneysen's resignation from the journal.[58]

Yet one finds in *Der Roemerbrief* ample evidence that Barth, too, had been drawn into a negative natural theology of existentialism. He explicitly linked faith to the radical self-questioning of the existential ego—using these very terms—and suggested that God could be found elsewhere than in Christ.[59] Consequently, Nicholls is correct when he writes

> It is not, I think, a misleading generalization if we say that all of Barth's associates of the nineteen-twenties who afterward differed from him did so because they remained in essentially the same position they had originally shared with Barth, while he moved on to a position they could not accept.[60]

THE LEGITIMATION OF CRISIS

If the existential overtones of the theology of crisis were a large part of its popularity and success in the 1920s, they also contributed to a major difficulty in its position. The focus on existential thought does avoid the problem of making a particular historical epoch the bearer of a special revelation—although Barth is right that its use transforms revealed religion into natural religion. But its legitimation of crisis unintentionally undermines itself, obviating the redemptive power of the crisis.

Barth had argued that the true task of religion—as

opposed to the false task adopted in its idolatrous forms—is to make us confront the questionableness of life, the fragility and ambiguity of all the things we believe to be stable and unequivocal. It was in the state of brokenness, in the shattering of one's (false) presumptions to know how things are, that one is confronted with how things really are. "Truth" is found in the shattering of "truths." This experience of dissolution was explicitly linked to despair, by both Barth and others. One experiences the disruption and the annihilation of one's possibilities as a devastating occurrence, because one is constituted to want to believe—in Nietzsche's terms, one is built to interpret, to value, to make judgments and find the world meaningful. Yet the experience of despair is nonetheless good, because with the shattering of one's possibilities comes authentic existence, the openness of faith and love.

But in order to be shattered, one must first possess something that can be shattered. And in order for the dissolution of possibilities to serve as a great question mark, a disruption and break in the order of things, it must be something which is resisted, not sought after, something, in fact, which we try to avoid. The act of making crisis and its corresponding despair a good, something religiously and ethically valuable, however, also makes them things that one in some sense should seek out. But if one willingly acquiesces to the dissolution of one's possibilities, the effect of this dissolution is not traumatic or disruptive in the way it needs to be in order to serve as the vehicle of genuine religiosity. Helmut Kuhn has formulated the problem quite succinctly:

> By definition crisis can overtake only one who believes. But the anticipation of crisis is incompatible with belief. Hence by embracing a philosophy of crisis I acquire immunity from suffering a crisis. Consequently this philosophy, in a curious reversal of purpose, will tend to create complacency rather than fortitude.[61]

So effectively, in other words, does this move deal with

crisis that it wipes crisis out of existence. What was once a curse is now a blessing, and the negative connotations intrinsic to the meaning of crisis have vanished along with the anxiety. Could not one still have the positive benefits of crisis without its negative overtones? Clearly the locution is misleading. For crisis is a critical juncture, by definition, a kind of limiting point that cannot be made the center and ground of a position without changing its fundamental nature.

The dialectical theologians offered a quite skillful response to nihilism, appropriating the dissolution of Christianity for the benefit of faith. Religion is sacrificed that religiosity may persevere. Yet such effort ultimately is self-defeating, for as Kuhn has pointed out, by making the experience of nihilism and the crisis associated with it a feature of the basic make-up of human beings, it is divested of its power to shock. But the shock was precisely what was necessary for good to be done. The result of the existentialist legitimation of nihilism is precisely the banality of postmodernism.

Barth, at least, was aware of this latent difficulty. This is why he described his position as "no position," consistently resisting all attempts to make crisis the basis of a theological system. He wrote in 1922,

> I must frankly confess to you that what I might conceivably call "my theology" becomes, when I look at it closely, a single point, and that not, as one might demand as the least qualification of a true theology, a *stand*point, but rather a *mathematical* point upon which one cannot stand—a *view*point merely.[62]

One finds throughout *Der Roemerbrief* similar recourse to mathematical terminology to describe the non-spatial character of faith and revelation, i.e., their inability to be treated as things among other things in the world. Barth's rejection and disdain for natural theology stemmed from the recognition that humanly generated crisis would not work.

Such recognition notwithstanding, it is difficult in

hindsight not to read the theology of crisis as a kind of negative natural theology. A particular attitude, linked to the postwar experience, was appropriated and then made the sole basis of authentic religious affirmation. Nihilism was made holy as part of the gracious act of God. Thus Nietzsche's uncanniest of guests became, for a brief period of time, a divinely bestowed gift. But in consequence nihilism both ceases to be a temporary phenomenon, becoming instead the ahistorical horizon in which faith arises, and loses its ability to provoke the crisis necessary for its redemptive power.

5

Richard Rorty and the Dissolution of Crisis

THE POSTMODERN MOOD

The impact of dialectical theology proper was largely limited to the theological sphere; the ethos it expressed, however, was not. Existentialism, its secular analogue, became increasingly an object of attention throughout the next few decades. The works of Heidegger, Jaspers, Sartre, and Camus—as well as their nineteenth-century forebears, Nietzsche, Kierkegaard, and Dostoevsky—struck a responsive chord among many intellectuals in both Europe and America, culminating in the 1960s.[1] The combined impact of the First and Second World War, the fragmentation of even the nebulous religious unity of liberalism, and a tolerant relativism which often appeared to degenerate into anarchism, proved fertile ground for a view insisting that the confrontation with meaninglessness was a necessary component of genuine human existence.

Saved from a despairing dissolution by an insistence that nihilism was not the sole or final word, the move we saw earlier in Barth was echoed in Heidegger's analysis of *Dasein,* in Sartre's account of "bad faith" and the call for authenticity, and Camus' portrait of the absurd hero.

Sartre, in fact, suggested that, despite the "distress" accompanying the realization that there is no God (i.e., that no structure or power exists outside the individual consciousness to validate its decisions), recognizing this fact was the necessary precondition for authentic existence. Only then was the full burden of human resposibility placed on each individual's shoulders.[2] Being authentic meant taking full responsibility for one's actions, facing up to the truth that there is no truth other than the truth one wills, no ground or justification for this willing other than its own brute fact, coupled with a conviction of the seriousness of one's decisions, so that any particular act of willing is always made in a state of what Kierkegaard called "fear and trembling."

The existentialist sensibility—a preoccupation with the abyss opened up by God's abdication (or, if Nietzsche was right, by his murder)—still lingers on in corners of academia, but center stage is now dominated by a new and different intellectual current, widely if imprecisely known as "deconstruction." Represented in diverse academic fields, the thinkers generally labeled "deconstructionists" vary greatly in approach and technique, so much so that a variety of competing designations also exist.[3] What unites this wide-ranging group is a common contempt for all claims to have found definitive and unambiguous truth, value, or meaning, above and beyond any given field of discourse, and more important, a rejection of all attempts to continue to seek such truths, values, or meaning. The existentialist refrain that we have no access to any sure ground, foundation, or basis for our beliefs and actions has been retuned, in other words, transposed from a minor to a major key. The dissolution of foundations—a source of anxiety (or at least concern) for the existentialists—is now seen as a source of joyous affirmation, of lighthearted playfulness, or benign indifference.

A scholar attending a summer conference on postmodernism, reading the works of Foucault, Derrida, Richard Rorty, Harold Bloom, and others, described the underlying temper of this new movement:

> Many of the colleagues in the seminar and almost all of the books I was reading were urging me to abandon the ideal of truth, to laugh at the dream of hope, and to cease any search for meaning. To paraphrase a few of my summer colleagues: The bad news is that there is no good news, and the good news is, surprisingly, that there has never been any good news. So we are liberated by knowing that we have no right to lament the loss of something we never had. We need not be saved because we are not lost.[4]

What Richard Bernstein has called the "Cartesian anxiety"—the distress accompanying the realization that we may live in a "chaos where nothing is fixed, where we can neither touch bottom nor support ourselves on the surface"[5]—finds no point of entry with most deconstructionists. It is not that the anxiety has been exactly dissolved nor even assuaged. It has merely been set aside, as the product of a false and illusory quest: the search for absolute certainty, for secure foundations. In consequence, nihilism occasions not anxiety nor distress, nor the need for heightened strength and an increase in vigor, but either gleeful or bored acceptance, depending upon which variant of deconstruction one accepts. The threat of Nietzsche's "danger of dangers" has apparently been defused.

This shift in mood is both interesting and important: interesting, because it contrasts so sharply with the preceding two centuries; important, because it is reasonable to expect that such a shift in temperament is a reflection of a corresponding shift in the self-understanding of its proponents. While there has been little unanimity of opinion about the source of nihilism (or its cure), from its earliest coinage to the present day, it has, with only two exceptions, been regarded as something troubling, because it was seen as the loss of something believed fundamental to human life.[6] The fact that the advent of nihilism is seen as an occasion for cheer suggests that this appraisal of human need is no longer shared, and that therefore a different and presumably new ideal of human life informs contemporary reflection.

The so-called "deconstructive" turn in philosophy[7]

refers in part to this shift in temperament, in part to the philosophical strategies that ensue from it. The temperament is marked by what Jean-François Lyotard has called "incredulity towards meta-narratives." Such incredulity, Lyotard argues, is one of the defining characteristics of the contemporary intellectual scene. In his reading, modern—or more precisely, postmodern—intellectuals are abandoning the attempt to ground the particular truth claims of discrete fields of discourse in an overarching meta-theory of universal relevance. The Enlightenment goal of a universal community of rational beings no longer serves to orient their thinking. While earlier in this century the realization of the impossibility of this goal may have provoked grief, Lyotard remarks that "we can see today [i.e., 1979] that the mourning process has been completed.... Most people have lost the nostalgia for the lost narrative." This loss of nostalgia, and the corresponding absence of any distress over the missing narrative, is, according to Lyotard, "what the postmodern world is all about."[8]

Richard Rorty has been one of the most vocal apologists for this sensibility in the United States. While his views could hardly embody the full diversity of deconstruction, he represents—and perhaps initiated—a verson of it that has been quite popular in this country: anti-foundationalism.[9] Widely known for its indictment of traditional philosophical discourse, anti-foundationalism stresses our inability to move from our language and our beliefs to something behind or beyond that serves as a legitimating ground. This alone, of course, does not serve to distinguish anti-foundationalism—or for that matter, postmodernism—from earlier forms of thought. What does distinguish anti-foundationalism from movements predating it is the equanimity with which anti-foundationalists broadcast this fact and their apparent indifference to the consequences that follow from it. As we shall see, this equanimity not only has important implications for their understanding of nihilism, but serves as means of distinguishing different strands of the postmodern sensibility.

THE ANTI-FOUNDATIONALIST CRITIQUE OF PHILOSOPHY

From the early 1970s most of Rorty's work has been devoted to the criticism and debunking of a certain picture of philosophy: its self-understanding as a foundational discipline, one which sees itself as responsible for the maintenance and adjudication of a culture's claims to truth. Culture, according to Rorty, may be regarded as "the assemblage of claims to knowledge," where knowledge is understood as "accurate representation of what is outside the mind"; philosophy is traditionally perceived as the adjudication of such claims.[10] For most of the modern era, Rorty writes, philosophy

> was the one area of culture where one touched bottom, where one found the vocabulary and the convictions which permitted one to explain and to justify one's activity as an intellectual, and thus to discover the significance of one's life. (5-6)

Philosophy not only got at truth, but at Truth; it told us both what the world was like and how we knew the world was like that. By focusing on the mind and upon epistemology, it claimed relevance to all areas of what came to be known in the late nineteenth century as the *Geisteswissenschaften,* for it described and legitimated every bridge between the individual consciousness and the world in which this consciousness found itself, even describing the operations of this consciousness in isolation.

Part of Rorty's tale lies in showing how the rise of scientific paradigms of reasoning affected this self-understanding. The more "scientific" philosophy became, the more remote from the rest of culture it became at the same time, thereby losing its ability to maintain convincingly its role as chief adjudicator. But Rorty's more important point is concerned with showing how the correspondence theory of truth gradually lost credibility. This is central to his story, because the correspondence notion of truth was a foundation stone in the self-image of philosophy; it was this understanding of truth that made a certain kind of realist epistemology its stock in trade. As long as the general model of human inquiry was that there were two distinct things—a world "out there" and ideas (later, sentences, expressing propositions) "in here"—philosophy could portray itself as that branch of human reason which both understood and guided the mapping of the "inside" onto the "outside," the faithful correspondence of subjective perception with objective fact. Philosophers, in Rorty's eyes, were members of a conceptual Mafia, determining what sorts of claims could and could not be made; individual philosophers were hit men whose job was to eliminate false or spurious notions, judged by the standard of the reigning boss.

This kind of philosophic inquiry Rorty describes as "systematic," in comparison with another kind of philosophical enterprise, described as "edifying." If systematic philosophers are the hit men of the world of culture, edifying philosophers are the aerobics instructors, toning flabby motivations and strengthening self-images. Edifying philosophy, Rorty writes, is "designed to make the reader question his own motives for philosophizing, rather than to supply him with a new philosophical program." Edifying philosophers keep us honest: "The cultural role of the edifying philosopher is to help us avoid the self-deception which comes from believing that we know ourselves by knowing a set of objective factors" (373). Edifying philosophers, in other words, serve two purposes: They restrict the realm of any particular claim to have captured all of existence, thereby serving to offset the natural dogmatism of systematicians; and they preserve a sense that there is something more to us than any description could possibly capture—in the words of the intellectual heritage from which Rorty later takes pains to distinguish himself, they preserve *Geist*.

Thus Rorty's overall goal in *Philosophy and the Mirror of Nature* appears to be two-sided. He wishes, first, to argue that a certain understanding of philosophy will no longer work, that foundationalist epistemology has been demonstrated by its own defenders to be impossible. Second, he wishes to contrast the "systematic" impulse of such foundationalists—people committed to "the project of universal commensuration" (368)—with the "edifying" impulse of hermeneutic thinkers, who aim "at continuing a conversation rather than at discovering truth" (373).

The distinction between edifying and systematic thinkers is itself neither controversial nor revolutionary; the use Rorty appears to want to make of this distinction is also relatively tame. While Rorty clearly thinks the way in which the systematic impulse has been manifested in our own age—in the quest for a foundationalist epistemology—has proven abortive, and that the edifying alternatives of the later Wittgenstein, Heidegger, and Sartre are more valuable to us at the present time, this says nothing about the feasibility or integrity of the systematic impulse more generally, nor of the lasting value of various forms of existentialism or pragmatism. One is tempted to read Rorty in the vein of Thomas Kuhn, whose influence Rorty acknowledges: Systematic "normal" discourse and edifying "abnormal" discourse are simply two different sides of human inquiry, both of which are necessary for the progress of thinking.[11]

Rorty writes that edifying philosophy is "reactive, having sense only as a protest against attempts to close off conversation by proposals of universal commensuration through the hypostasization of some privileged set of descriptions" (377). Normal or systematic discourse attempts to offer comprehensive accounts of what life is like, what we hold to be true and good and why we should hold such beliefs; edifying philosophy prevents us from taking these convictions as more than temporary resting places in the "universal conversation of mankind," ensuring that we regard them, in the terminology of William James, as "practical prescriptions for use." It prevents the ugly reification of contingent fact into absolute truth. Or, as Rorty puts it,

> The danger which edifying discourse tries to avert is that some given vocabulary, some way in which people might

> come to think of themselves, will deceive them into thinking that from now on all discourse could be, or should be, normal discourse. The resulting freezing-over of culture would be, in the eyes of edifying philosophers, the dehumanization of human beings. (377)

In passages like this, Rorty seems to argue that edifying philosophy is above all else a guarantee of openness and toleration against dogmatism and absolutism. And while the tenor of *Philosophy and the Mirror of Nature* suggests that a certain kind of foundationalist realism has had its day, there is no reason to suggest that the systematic urge more generally be uprooted. To do so would be simultaneously to undercut the possibility of edifying discourse, and, by extension, of thinking in general.

That Rorty (at least in *Philosophy and the Mirror of Nature*) does not wish to present his own interpretation of the nature of philosophical reflection as particularly controversial or revolutionary is evident from both his desire to connect his reading with the heritage of the Enlightenment and his frequent positive appeal to earlier thinkers from both the systematic and edifying camps. The openness and absence of dogmatism the presence of edifying philosophy ensures is explictly linked to the moral and scientific ideals of the eighteenth century. We can—indeed, should—abandon the particular way Enlightenment thinkers went about their project, in the interest of preserving the underlying ethos that motivated it. Rorty writes,

> The fact that the Enlightenment ran together the ideal of the autonomy of science from theology and politics with the image of scientific theory as Mirror of Nature is not a reason for preserving this confusion. The grid of relevance and irrelevance which we inherit almost intact from the eighteenth century will be more attractive when it is no longer tied to this image. Shopworn mirror metaphors are of no help in keeping intact the inheritance—both moral and scientific—of Galileo. (333)

Rorty accepts the idea "that the preservation of the values of the Enlightenment is our best hope" (335–6), noting parenthetically that such a conviction is "entirely justified,"[12] but feels that to continue this project in its own terms is the wrong way to go about it.[13] What we need to do is recognize the provisional character of our belief systems in light of a trans-historical commitment to integrity, honesty, toleration. It is the edifying philosopher who enables us to do this, in cooperation with the systematic philosopher, by continually casting doubt upon the whole project offered by the systematician.

Thus interpreted, Rorty's remarks here are, by and large, unexceptional, and it is difficult to understand how the book could have caused the degree of controversy it did.[14] True, Rorty closes with the comment, "Perhaps philosophy will become purely edifying"—puzzling in light of his insistence, just pages before, that edifying philosophy is by definition reactive. But he follows this immediately with the speculation "Perhaps a new form of systematic philosophy will be found which has nothing whatever to do with epistemology but which nevertheless makes normal philosophical inquiry possible" (394). Nothing he has said, he continues, makes one possibility more plausible than the other.[15]

Yet Rorty's other published writings, written both before and after the appearance of *Philosophy and the Mirror of Nature* belie this evenhanded, tempered view of the nature of philosophical inquiry. Many of these essays are collected in a book entitled *Consequences of Pragmatism.*[16] The introduction to that volume is particularly illuminating, for it provides a less ambiguous statement of Rorty's views, as well as a programmatic sketch of what he would like to see happen in our intellectual life.

The issue in that essay is no longer the preservation of two types of philosophy, but the clear-cut abandonment of "Philosophy"—broadened to include almost all philosophical reflection after Plato—in favor of what Rorty calls a "post-Philosophical culture." The older "Philosophy" (as opposed to "philosophy") is committed to "the impossible attempt to step outside our skins...and compare ourselves with something absolute."[17] Rorty derides this desire for transcendence as "a metaphysical urge," and regards it as something we would be better off without. Why? Quite simply, because "attempts to get back behind language to something which 'grounds' it or which it 'expresses' or to which it might hope to be 'adequate' have not worked" (xx). The most recent area of philosophy that promised to offer such bedrock notions—the Anglo-American analytic tradition—according to Rorty, has only been able to "transcend and cancell itself" in the work of Quine, the later Wittgenstein, Sellars, and Davidson (xviii).

Rorty has thus broadened his attack to include not only the epistemological foundationalism of the last three centuries, but any attempt to find a ground or a foundation outside of the particular community of discourse in which we happen to find ourselves, arguing that we should simply "not ask questions about the nature of Truth and Goodness" any longer (xiv). Stressing that this rejection is not itself a position or a theory, Rorty describes himself as someone who simply is not interested in offering theories about truth or goodness—or about anything else, for that matter. The desire to offer a theory betrays precisely the kind of commitment to foundationalism that Rorty claims not to have. Thus, while Rorty's remarks in *Philosophy and the Mirror of Nature* suggest that systematic philosophy has its fruits to offer, the Rorty one finds in other works clearly does not think so.[18] Such theoretical inclinations are passé, and should be rooted out along with the outmoded fashions in our closets.

Precisely this criticism and rejection of a certain kind of philosophy (foundationalist or metaphysical epistemology), coupled with his conviction that the history of philosophy drives itself to this realization[19] is Rorty's entrance ticket to the halls of deconstruction. He seems in many ways the personification of Lyotard's "incredulity toward meta-narratives" described above, the American equivalent of Jacques Derrida, the Continental excesses of the latter steeped and purified in a hearty U.S. pragmatism. Rorty himself acknowledges the ties between his thinking and Derrida's in his 1980 essay, "Nineteenth-Century Idealism and Twentieth-Century Textualism." Yet by 1984, the differences between their positions appear to be more striking to him than the similarities he had earlier identified.

Rorty's desire to differentiate himself from Derrida is especially important for our purposes—despite the fact that it mandates a brief detour into the pitfalls of Derrida's thought—since the point that separates them is, as we shall see, the degree of seriousness with which each views the move away from foundationalist, "presentist" views of discourse. This, in turn, is linked to the interpretation and significance which each gives to nihilism.[20]

DECONSTRUCTION, *DIFFÉRANCE*, AND PLAY

Like Rorty, Derrida was trained as a philosopher; also like Rorty, his relationship to philosophy has become increasingly tenuous as his criticisms of it become more pronounced, and his works have found a more receptive home among other disciplines, primarily literary criticism.[21] Unlike Rorty, however, Derrida has maintained his position on a philosophical faculty,[22] a difference which is mirrored in their appraisal of the nature of philosophy more generally. Although both agree that philosophical thought has for centuries been misled by a dream which it cannot possibly hope to fulfill and that the admission of the impossibility of this is an occasion for relief, if not celebration, Rorty ultimately wishes to distinguish his response to this event from Derrida's; while lauding Derrida's apparent rejection of the pompous self-importance that has characterized so much of philosophical reflection in the past, in the final analysis, Rorty regards Derrida as still trapped by the lure of foundationionalism.

Despite Derrida's role as the founder of a new kind of literary criticism, the subject of almost all of his writings is philosophy, which he understands as a discipline that always attempts to "say its own limit," that is, to be all-encompassing, self-grounding, or foundational.[23] He seeks a place from which he can criticize philosophy (i.e., provide a critique in the traditional sense) without himself being enmeshed in the pitfalls of philosophical discourse. He seeks, in his own words, "a non-philosophical place, a place of exteriority or alterity from which one might still treat *of philosophy*." Yet he acknowledges that this is, strictly speaking, a doomed enterprise, for philosophy always and everywhere "appropriates" its "exteriority." The point here, Derrida's somewhat strained terminology aside, is that philosophical discourse, by its very nature, imposes itself upon any and every attempt at criticism, whether the critic be conscious of this, or no. Any position—including the most rigidly anti-metaphysical—has a metaphysical underpinning. Indeed, Derrida suggests that our thinking itself is necessarily metaphysical, so that he "do[es] not believe that someday it will be possible simply to escape metaphysics."[24]

Consequently, it is more correct to say that Derrida speaks on the borders or fringes of philosophical discourse rather than outside of it. He writes, "I try to keep myself at the *limit* of philosophical discourse."[25] This explains why he pays such an extraordinary amount of attention to offhand remarks, fragments, footnotes, obscure texts deemed trivial or uninteresting by the tradition, as well as why he jumps, in an almost arbitrary fashion, from topic to topic. We may liken him to the night sentry who is capable of seeing only by keeping his eyes continually moving over the horizon: To stare fixedly at any one point is to give oneself up into darkness. It is only through peripheral vision that one can see at all.

Despite his apparent erratic intellectual style, Derrida's thought is closely organized around four foci. First, he wishes to show that philosophy has been dominated by a certain vision of meaning as presence, as fully disclosed being, as immediacy. Second, he argues that this domination undermines itself, for a careful examination of any philosophical text shows that presence is always deferred. There is no immediacy (i.e., no direct confrontation with the object of language); there are only signs that stand in for immediacy. Any philosophical text (or indeed, any text at all) reveals only a closed chain of signifiers that points only to itself, never to anything external to it. Third, he attempts to provide an account of meaning that is not predicated upon a link to being, presence, immediacy, one grounded in the differential play of signs among themselves rather than in reference to some external origin. Fourth, he tries to suggest an appropriate response to the "rupture" in thought that takes place when the absence of meaning as fully disclosed being is recognized. His thought is difficult to understand (much less describe) because it does not proceed in a linear or straightforward fashion; rather, each of these concerns is woven together, at times one coming to the fore, at other times, another.

His most extended book is *Of Grammatology*, the final goal of which is "to make enigmatic what one thinks one understands by the words 'proximity,' 'immediacy,' 'presence'" (70). Thus he desires to undermine what he takes to be the decisive presumption of philosophical discourse in the West: the conviction that there is some fundamental ground, some "transcendental signified" that it is the goal of any system of signs to point to and to reveal. The meaning of any system of signs is measured in terms of its adequacy as a fulcrum of revelation for this signified transcendental; Derrida defines "logocentrism" or "the metaphysics of presence" as "the exigent, powerful, systematic, and irrepressible desire for such a signified" (49).

The problem with such a desire, though, is that we simply have no access to the transcendental signified, or indeed, to *any* original signified whatever. "There is...no phenomenality reducing the sign or the representer so that the thing signified may be allowed to glow finally in the luminosity of its presence" (49). We have only signs that refer to other signs that refer to other signs, and so forth. There is no way for us to break out of this infinite chain, for we "think only in signs" (50). Signs are what give us meaning, but we have mistakenly attributed the source of this meaning to the adequacy of their representative function. This cannot be the source since we have no access to a thing in itself, yet we nonetheless do appear to have meaning.

Derrida attempts to explain the possibility of meaning by means of a modification of Saussure's account of the interdependence of signs.[26] Signs have meaning only in the context of an entire system. No sign, removed from the system of interplay in which it is enmeshed, is sensible. Derrida coins the word *"différance"* (changing the "e" of the French word *différence* to an "a") to describe, in part, the acquisition of meaning through the interplay of signs. The concept of *différance* ties together two ideas. First, the meaning of any particular sign is dependent upon its difference, its quality of being different, from other signs. Difference indicates uniqueness, hence meaning. Second, because the interplay of signs is in perpetual movement, the possibility of any ultimate or definitive meaning is always deferred to a later date.[27]

The meaning or meanings engendered by the interplay of signs Derrida calls a "trace." The trace is what loosely binds together any system of signs, so that at any one moment, a given sign works by referring to other signs not now present. To quote Derrida,

> The play of differences supposes, in effect, syntheses and referrals which forbid at any moment, or in any sense, that a simple element be *present* in and of itself, referring only to itself.
>
> This interweaving [of signs] results in each "element" being constituted on the basis of the trace within it of the other elements of the chain or system. This interweaving, this textile, is the *text* produced only in the transformation of another text. Nothing, neither among the elements nor within the system, is anywhere ever simply present or absent. There are only, everywhere, differences and traces of traces.[28]

Derrida's stated goal is to attempt to wrest meaning from the stranglehold of logocentrism and its "ontotheological" death grip. He wishes to kill the obsession we have with origins, arguing that in the play of representation "the point of origin becomes ungraspable. There are things like reflecting pools, and images, an infinite reference from one to the other, but no longer a source, a spring. There is no longer a simple origin" (*Grammatology*, 36). The desire for origin is, at root, theological, for it seeks a fundament, a base, a transcendental upon which thinking can rest. In opposition to this, Derrida glorifies play, the play of representations, and the play of interpretations of these representations. By "play" Derrida means "the absence of the transcendental signified"; the "limitlessness of play" reflects "the destruction of onto-theology and the metaphysics of presence" (*Grammatology*, 50).

The fundamental goal of Derrida's work can thus be construed as emancipatory, for he wishes to free us from an understanding of the world and of our relationship to it that is restrictive, if not plainly false.[29] He links his enterprise explicitly to transformation: "an internal critique or deconstruction" is an "essential part" of any culture's development, for "every culture needs an element of self-interrogation and of distance from itself, if it is to transform itself."[30] Yet he rejects the claim that with his focus on *différance* and absence he has offered us, in effect, a negative theology, thereby implying that there is no "transcendental signified." In the world transformed,

> There will be no unique name, even if it were the name of Being. And we must think this without *nostalgia*.... On the contrary, we must *affirm* this, in the sense in which Nietzsche puts affirmation into play, in a certain laughter and a certain step of the dance.[31]

Derrida resists all attempts beyond this to articulate what a more appropriate understanding of the world and of the self would be. At times, like Nietzsche, he suggests that a new epoch is dawning of which he is merely an early prophet. At other times, if more cryptically, the suggestion is made that it is already here, Derrida's own work being an example of what post-presentist reflection should yield. And at still other times, he suggests that no supercession of philosophy is possible, that all he seeks to do is to prevent the reification of particular philosophical concepts.

POSTMODERNIST BOURGEOIS LIBERALISM[32]

In an essay from 1980/81, Rorty notes approvingly that "textualism"—his name for the approach to cultural works employed by Derrida and his followers—is nineteenth-century idealism purged of the latter's metaphysical pretensions. It expresses the genuine insight of idealism—that thought and language are primary and cannot be "gotten behind," so to speak, for they "create," in a very real sense, the world in which they move—without making idealist statements about absolute *Geist* or the noumenal realm. Consequently, Rorty sees it as close to his own position:

> When philosophers like Derrida say things like "There is nothing outside the text," they are not making theoretical remarks, remarks backed up by epistemological or semantical arguments. Rather, they are saying, cryptically and aphoristically, that a certain framework of interconnected ideas—truth as correspondence, language as picture, literature as imitation—ought to be abandoned. They are not, however, claiming to have discovered the *real* nature of truth or language or literature. Rather, they are saying that the very notion of discovering the *nature* of such things is part of the intellectual framework which we must abandon—part of what Heidegger calls the "metaphysics of presence" or the "onto-theological tradition."[33]

Derrida, in other words, is simply the Continental equivalent of Rorty himself. Without knowing it, textualism is nothing other than "an attempt to think through a thoroughgoing pragmatism, a thoroughgoing abandonment of the notion of *discovering the truth* which is common to theology and science."[34] Scratch Derrida, says Rorty, and you will find William James.

Yet by 1984 Rorty wants to distance himself from Derrida. Derrida has himself fallen prey to a kind of self-aggrandizing self-deception. "The big esoteric problem," Rorty writes, "common to Heidegger and Derrida of how to 'overcome' or escape from the onto-theological tradition is an artificial one."[35] To view metaphysics as something which must be overcome (and therefore, by implication, nihilism in a bad sense as something that ensues from its dissolution) is to have failed to learn the pragmatist lesson: Truth is nothing more than a particular community's understanding of what is good in the way of belief. Derrida produces "a new metalinguistic jargon"; his attempts "to give arguments for such theses as 'Writing is prior to speech' or 'Texts deconstruct themselves'...betray his own project" (9). Thus Rorty sees Derrida as someone whose motivations are perhaps sound, but who is still caught up in a framework that makes the useful implementation of such motivations impossible. The key indication of this framework is the seriousness with which Derrida takes his project. There is, says Rorty, "a tone of urgency" surrounding Derrida's works which "is out of place" (19), out of place because, properly viewed, the problems prompting such urgency can simply be set aside.

In part this urgency stems from Derrida's conviction that he is doing something both important and serious because, as we saw above, Derrida regards some kind of deconstructive (or, to use the language of *Philosophy and the Mirror of Nature,* "edifying") enterprise as a necessary component in cultural transformation. Derrida rejects, as we have also seen, the possibility that metaphysics could ever simply "come to an end," and therefore can be regarded as viewing deconstructive work as a part of a more overarching metaphysical project, or rather, as part of that enterprise of which metaphysics is also a part—the overall project of human inquiry and reflection. While Derrida never expresses himself along quite these lines,[36] Rorty's criticisms suggest that this is what he thinks Derrida is really saying. By 1984, Rorty regards Derrida's thinking as possessing a covert realism, a realism that is out of synch with both the claims and goal of deconstruction.

One way of understanding the difference between Derrida and Rorty, as well as the difference more generally between realism and Rorty's version of pragmatism, is in terms of a clash of intuitions about how the world is and should be. Rorty distinguishes his neo-pragmatic view from that of the realists precisely in this way in the previously mentioned introduction to *Consequences of Pragmatism.* Conceding that many people are convinced that there must be some intelligibility to the notion of objective or independent truth, to the existence of some ground or foundation to the patterns of speech and inference we employ, Rorty suggests that such intuitions are simply a product of the firm grasp certain forms of realism have had in the West. "*Of course* we have such intuitions," he exclaims; "How could we escape having them? We have been educated within an intellectual tradition built around such claims" (xxix). We have been taught, in other words, to regard alethiological nihilism as an anathema. But the pragmatist "is a pragmatist just because he doesn't have such intuitions (or wants to get rid of whatever such intuitions he may have)" (xxviii).

Rorty continues by suggesting that the intuitive realist and the pragmatist may simply have "been born with different metaphysical temperaments,"[37] but this is quickly amended. The real issue is not whether there are people who have realist intuitions, or a metaphysical urge—even Rorty himself apparently has them, as the above quotation suggests—but whether "we must find a philosophical view which 'captures' such intuitions." "The pragmatist," Rorty claims, "is urging that we do our best to *stop having* such intuitions, that we develop a *new* intellectual tradition" (xxx).[38]

Seen against this background, we can infer that the tone of "urgency" Rorty finds "out of place" in the writings of Derrida is indeed a function of this misbegotten metaphysical urge still operative in his thinking. This metaphysical tendency, which appears linked implicitly in Rorty's mind to the systemetizing form of philosophy he describes in *Philosophy and the Mirror of Nature*, is more directly evident in Derrida's attempts to offer a "metalinguistic" explanation for his more erratic claims. Derrida is right to be overtly suspicious of the realist claim, yet his attempt to ground his attack in a theory of meaning derived from Saussure is at odds with this suspicion. To do so is implicitly to throw in his lot with those who practice "Philosophy."

This difference Rorty sees between his own outlook and that of Derrida reflects more generally the difference between the traditional understanding of philosophical discourse and the new alternative Rorty wishes to pose. Not surprisingly, since the appearance of *Philosophy and the Mirror of Nature* in 1979, Rorty has written at length seeking to delineate this difference as clearly as possible. We have already seen that the original distinction between "systematic" and "edifying" was almost immediately recast in terms of "Philosophy" (bad) and "philosophy" (good), and that this is illustrated more concretely by means of the distinction between "realists" and "pragmatists." Rorty also casts the difference in terms of a distinction between "objectivity" and "solidarity."[39]

Those thinkers who see solidarity as fundamental—the pragmatists—seek to reduce the notion of truth as correspondence with some objective reality to the idea of truth as an expression of communal utility. "They view truth as, in William James' phrase, what it is good for *us* to believe" (5). Realists, by contrast, seek to ground any communal sense of truth in objectivity, which forces them to "construct a metaphysics which has room for a special relation between beliefs and objects which will differentiate true from false beliefs" (5). Rorty's point here is that those thinkers who seek "objectivity" for their beliefs are required to build elaborate metaphysical and epistemological edifices not only to describe the reality their beliefs seek to capture but also to clarify how they distinguish true from false beliefs. Those who seek "solidarity," by contrast, need only to appeal to the communal warrants and norms currently operative in a community to justify any particular claim to knowledge or to adjudicate between competing claims.

The implications of Rorty's view are most fully spelled out in a little-known essay called "Hermeneutics, General Studies, and Teaching,"[40] in which Rorty considers what education would look like if it started from the presumption that Nietzsche, not Plato, was correct—if, in other words, we regarded truth as the function of community agreement rather than objective validity.[41] The fundamental task in this case would be, according to Rorty, trying to inculcate "intellectual hero worship" in students, i.e., trying to instill in others a love and respect for those thinkers we have found to be the most worthy of study and emulation. The goal should be openly pluralistic—"to make sure that no student has only *one* hero"—thereby offsetting the potential dangers of dogmatism; the means should be openly seductive. The point is to socialize students into the community that we take to be the most valuable and worthwhile, to introduce them to the thinkers who have most contributed to our understanding of who we are and what we should do. "The content of core curricula is whatever books the most influential members of the faculty of a given institution all happen to have liked, or all like to teach—the books which give them the greatest pleasure" (12).

Thus, instead of some outmoded ideal of truth as corresponding to the way things "really" are, Rorty would have us acknowledge that all of our truth claims are both historically transmitted and historically conditioned. Our claims to know the world are really nothing more than an expression of how we—a particular group of people, or, as Rorty puts it above, the "most influential" people—take the world to be. These claims reflect nothing of the deep structure of the universe, nor do they reveal any timeless or cosmic truths. In the post-Philosophical culture that Rorty envisions, "men and women [feel] themselves alone, merely finite, with no links to something Beyond."[42] But such a feeling need not prompt despair, for the "reflective mind" has the option of "accepting the contingent character" of our belief systems. This gives us "a renewed sense of community...with our society, our political tradition, our intellectual heritage."[43] Rather than promoting alienation and *angst,* in other words, the recognition of the relative, contingent nature of human thought and action can heighten our sense of membership with other men and women and provide us with a kind of security forever lacking in the search for some transcendental ground. All we need to do is relinquish a standard for truth that no one has any idea how to fulfill.

DECONSTRUCTING NIHILISM

Despite their differences, both deconstruction and anti-foundationalism are frequently charged with nihilism.[44] This is not surprising, since both deny that we have or can hope to have access to some ground or certitude beyond that found in particular spheres of discourse (whether this be texts or communities); both deny that talk of such a ground is even intelligible. Such (negative) assertions invite the adjective "nihilistic," since they can be read as denying the possibility of knowledge, of truth, of ethics, or of a world existing independently of language. Thus four of the five strands of nihilism described above seem to loom large on the postmodern horizon.[45]

The response to this charge, however, can only be described as ambivalent. On the one hand, there is a certain amount of concern to defray it, suggesting that postmodern thinkers share the appraisal of their critics that nihilism is something undesirable. This appraisal is also implied in Derrida's concern with the "rupture" in thought that deconstruction provokes. Yet, on the other hand, after the dust has settled, there is a kind of indifferent acceptance, as though, properly understood, nihilism is not a significant concern and should not be made out to be such.

This attitude of rather bland indifference perhaps

explains in part the curious scarcity of sustained attempts to respond to the accusations. The disclaimers are generally limited to short, offhand remarks or outrage that such a "misreading" has occurred.[46] Derrida nowhere addresses this issue, to my knowledge,[47] but J. Hillis Miller, an American advocate of deconstruction, has discussed the relationship between deconstruction and nihilism at some length in "The Critic as Host."[48] Rorty's responses, too, are surprisingly circumspect, found primarily in "Pragmatism, Relativism, Irrationalism" and "Solidarity or Objectivity?", as well as in passing in *Contingency, Irony, and Solidarity.*

Miller's essay nicely illustrates the ambivalence of deconstruction's relation to nihilism. While he explicitly acknowledges that "nihilism...has inevitably come up as a label for 'deconstruction,'" he claims that nihilism is something to be feared only from the standpoint of metaphysical thinking. Only if metaphysics is viewed as the primary discipline (the "host," in the biological sense) can nihilism (the "parasite") be regarded as some kind of disease, infection, or degradation of it. If one inverts the relationship, making nihilism the primary term, the nasty connotations associated with it would inevitably disappear—or, more precisely, they would be transferred to metaphysics, metaphysics then becoming the parasite. "Deconstruction," Miller writes, "is one current name for this reversal." "Anti-foundationalism" would be another.

Thus here it appears that the goal of deconstruction is to embrace nihilism by making it primary. In doing so, we get rid of the basis for any objections we might have to it. This is a variation on the time-honored strategy of giving in to the inevitable: if one finds nihilism to be an uncanny guest, merely offer it full-time residence, and your appraisal of it will change. The problem with this response, of course, is that the uncanny features of nihilism remain, whether we regard it as guest or chief occupant. So, not surprisingly, Miller rejects such an explanation as quickly as he offers it: "'Deconstruction' is neither nihilism nor metaphysics but simply interpretation as such, the untangling of the inherence of metaphysics in nihilism and of nihilism in metaphysics by way of the close reading of texts" (230). This suggests that the deconstructive critic operates from some privileged place, outside of either nihilism or metaphysics, calmly pointing out the parasitic relationship between the two.

However, this, too, is wrong: "Deconstruction does not provide an escape from nihilism, nor from metaphysics, nor from their uncanny inherence in one another. There is no escape. It does, however, move back and forth within this inherence" (231). Hence it is not that nihilism is a parasite on metaphysics, or metaphysics on nihilism; rather, these are two names for essentially the same thing, or for two moments of the same thing—human thought. The interesting and, no doubt, unintended consequence is that deconstruction itself becomes the parasite, feeding off the movement of human thought.

Miller's response to the problem of nihilism's relationship to deconstruction, in other words, is to play with the terms in a dizzying and confusing fashion, until the final, tentative conclusion is offered: Deconstruction is not nihilism, it merely identifies a nihilism that both exists and is an inevitable and intrinsic part of human reflection. If the deconstructionists are nihilists, then so are we all.

Rorty's move is in some ways similar, although presented in a more discursive fashion. He concedes that the most serious objections to views like his (here labeled "textualism") are moral, in that they appear to legitimate an "Anything-goes" mentality and, with it, the most pernicious form of relativism, a form logically indistinct from ethical and epistemological nihilism.[49] One prong of Rorty's defense of his own position is to attempt to distinguish it from the vicious forms of relativism it seems to entail.

In "Solidarity or Objectivity?" Rorty distinguishes between three possible meanings of relativism: (1) the view that "every belief is as good as every other" (essentially the epistemological nihilism described in Chapter Two), (2) the view that "'truth' is an equivocal term, having as many meanings as there are procedures of justification," (3) the view that "there is nothing to be said about either truth or rationality apart from descriptions of the familiar procedures of justification which a given society—*ours*—uses in one or another area of inquiry." This third view Rorty identifies as "ethnocentrism," and claims that only in this third sense can pragmatism legitimately be labeled relativistic.

Pragmatism does not argue that "anything goes" (the first meaning of relativism given above), because it continually appeals to the communal framework that underwrites any particular claim to the truth. There are definite, specifiable criteria within our community that we use to determine what we will call true and what we will call false. Thus, his view should not be seen as espousing epistemological nihilism, for he believes that knowledge claims can be made and standards and criteria exist within each community to which its members can appeal.

Pragmatism is not relativistic in the second sense, because it argues that there is a cross-cultural functional similarity in the way the word "truth" is used: "true" is always used as an honorific, "an expression of commendation." The specific content of truth claims will vary, of course, from culture to culture, but the way the word functions, i.e., as denoting a statement believed to be "good to believe," is everywhere the same. To quote Rorty: "The term 'true,' on [the pragmatist's] account, means the same in all cultures, just as equally flexible terms like 'here,' 'there,' 'good,' 'bad,' 'you,' and 'me' mean the same in all cultures.... The identity of meaning is...compatible with diversity of reference, and with diversity of procedures for assigning the terms" (6).

It is worth noting that Rorty is making an absolutist claim, namely, that regardless of the culture, the word "true" always functions in the same way, making pragmatism the opposite of relativism. This move is continued in Rorty's questioning of the equation of ethnocentrism (a more accurate characterization of pragmatism, in Rorty's eyes) with relativism proper. Really to be relativistic, Rorty argues, means that one holds that something—

usually truth—is relative to something else. But since the pragmatist is making no positive claim at all, according to Rorty, but merely the negative one—we should stop thinking about truth in a transcendental way and instead should simply employ the canons of justification already operative in our culture—he is making no assertion about anything being relative to anything else. The pragmatist's ethnocentrism is simply an expression of the fact that we are unable to get out of our own skins, that we see the world in a certain way, regard certain things as true and others as false because we cannot but do so, given the community in which we find ourselves, and the fact that our beliefs about the world are molded and shaped by the community.

Rorty's response is further developed in "Hermeneutics, General Studies, and Teaching," where he insists that vulgar relativism is a function of a false dichotomy, a belief that either there is absolute truth or there is utter nihilism. But, he claims, "our having no organ for truth, no Reason in the Platonic sense, does not mean that everything must be turned over to the emotions.... There is a middle way between reliance on a God-surrogate and on one's individual preferences—namely, reliance on the common sense of the community to which one belongs" (6). This is the way in which human reflection has always conducted itself, self-consciously or not, and therefore should neither be feared or indicted.

Rorty's defense of his position raises a number of questions. Consider, for example, his assertions about the semantics of the word "true." Is he making a descriptive claim about how we in fact use the word "true"? Or is he making a prescriptive claim that we would be better off if we all became pragmatists and started using "true" to mean "good in the way of belief"? Rorty would be the last person to deny that many people don't think that what they mean by "true" is exhaustively defined by "good in the way of belief"; he acknowledges that the realists are one group that "cannot believe that anybody would seriously deny that truth has an intrinsic nature," as we have already seen (see p. 102). This means that either Rorty's descriptive claims are the expression of one (small) community's understanding of truth—not the expression of how an entire culture or all cultures use the word—or that he is arguing that the realists are self-deceived. They think they are using "truth" to refer to some objective state of things, but in fact, they, too, are merely being pragmatists, and we would all be better off if we stopped pretending otherwise.

Rorty makes no clear statement one way or the other on this issue. The omission is understandable, since he cannot claim that his view is either a description of how things are, or a kind of epistemological therapy, without appealing to some "bottom line"—without, in other words, committing the same kind of mistake he has spent the last ten years trying to correct. The most charitable reading of his position (and one which he repeatedly insists is acccurate) is that he is not trying to make any kind of claim at all; he is simply offering a prudential piece of advice: We should stop trying to look for things we are never going to find and concentrate instead on more productive questions.[50]

Thus Rorty takes great pains to show that questioning traditional understandings of truth does not commit the questioner to the anarchy of epistemological nihilism. Eliminating "truth talk" does not eliminate discussions about what we can and cannot be said to know, for our canons of justification and warranted assertability are unaffected by such a move. Knowledge, in other words, is unaffected by the Rortyian project. So far, so good; but as we have seen, epistemological nihilism is only one strand of nihilism—what of its other forms?

In the opening of *Contingency, Irony, and Solidarity*—a work which continues his project not by making arguments for his views but by trying "to make the vocabulary I favor look attractive" (9)—Rorty writes,

> We need to make a distinction between the claim that the world is out there and the claim that truth is out there. To

> say that the world is out there, that it is not our creation, is to say, with common sense, that most things in space and time are the effects of causes which do not include human mental states. To say that truth is not out there is simply to say that where there are no sentences there is no truth, that sentences are elements of human languages, and that human languages are human creations. (5)

Here Rorty clearly wishes to avoid any equation between his position and metaphysical nihilism—while his views seem, in many regards, closer to idealism than to realism, he does not intend to deny the reality of an external world existing independently of our language and thought. Yet with the same stroke he seems to have unhesitatingly identified himself as an alethiological nihilist, with his claim that truth is "not out there."

Rorty would no doubt resist such a description of his views. He writes, "To say that we should drop the idea of truth as out there waiting to be discovered is not to say that we have discovered that, out there, there is no truth. It is to say that our purposes would be served best by ceasing to see truth as a deep matter, as a topic of philosophical interest, or 'true' as a term which repays 'analysis'" (8). As he has said countless times before, he is simply not interested in talking about truth, in offering any sort of theory or position on this subject. And this, he would say, should not be construed as a commitment to the theory that there is no truth. He simply wants to change the subject.[51]

This response, however, is hardly adequate to turn aside the charge of nihilism. More is needed than a simple rejection of the characterization—one needs to offer an argument. Rorty needs to show us how his view that "truth is not out there," how his constant claims that we have "no organ for truth," is not a form of alethiological nihilism. He needs to show, in other words, how his view differs meaningfully from a view explicitly stating that there is no truth.

One difference he could point to is that alethiological

nihilism is overtly contradictory, while his position is not. Straightforward assertions that there is no truth are guilty of philosophical incoherence; someone who says nothing whatever on that matter, however, cannot be accused of incoherence. Incoherence implies speech, and on the question of truth Rorty is silent. There is a big difference between offering a *theory* of (the absence of) truth and refraining from making any theoretical remarks at all.

While it is surely correct that it is one thing to offer a theory, another to refrain from talking altogether, it is not clear how that helps Rorty here. As we have already noted, nihilism—in any of its forms—is often not a carefully thought out position or theory; in consequence, Rorty cannot appeal to his aversion to theory as a way to avoid the label, for one can be an alethiological nihilist without holding any theory about the unreality of truth. To be sure, he has avoided the philosophical incoherence that attends straightforward statements of alethiological nihilism, but for all that is the impact or implication of his view any different? Practically speaking, what is the difference between saying "truth is not out there" and "there is no truth"?

One difference might be that when we claim that "truth is not out there," we might in effect be urging a different view of truth; we might be saying, for example, that truth is "in here," whatever that might mean. One thing such a comment could mean is that truth is a product of the epistemological procedures that define and constrain a particular community's discourse. Truth, in other words, is what we make it, according to the rules of our language game, not something outside of or extrinsic to the game that we must strive for. Sometimes Rorty does indeed speak as though this were his view, for example, when he criticize attempts "to make truth something more than what Dewey called 'warranted assertability': more than what one's peers will, *ceteris paribus*, let one get away with saying."[52] Here Rorty seems to be saying that the true is the justified—that if we understand what justified belief is, we understand what true belief is. Truth is intrinsic to the process of justification.

Far from saving Rorty's position from alethiological nihilism, though, this seems to usher it firmly toward that stance. If there is no distinction between justified belief and true belief, if "true" is simply another way of saying "justified," then the notion of truth seems to have dropped out of the picture altogether. With it has also disappeared the notion of false belief as anything more than unjustified belief. If "true" and "justified" mean the same thing, then no false justified beliefs are possible. The words "true" and "false" might as well be excised from our language.

Perhaps, though, this entire chain of reasoning is mistaken. After all, Rorty has repeatedly insisted that he is not offering any theory of truth, so to claim that he believes truth to be warranted assertability (regardless of casual comments he may have made to this effect) is unfair. How many times must he say it? Let's simply stop talking about truth, and worry instead about more useful problems. But this too seems, practically speaking, to devolve into alethiological nihilism. What is the difference between not talking about truth—especially when one's silence is as loud as Rorty's is—and believing that there is no truth to talk about? To my eyes, none; in both cases truth ceases to be an operative concern in our language and our reflection.

Note, however, that the alethiological nihilism implicit in Rorty's view does not entail the existential nihilism that ambivalently blessed both Nietzsche and Barth. Anxiety or despair over our inability to connect with capital-T Truth is silly, in Rorty's eyes, since there is no such Truth for us to connect with; why berate or bemoan our inability to do something that is impossible because its goal is nonexistent? Rorty's position, thus interpreted, appears to have common sense on its side: Why *should* people keep trying to do something that seems impossible? Indeed, why would they? It seems that we would in fact be better off leaving this particular brick wall behind us.

On closer scutiny, however, this solution seems not so simple. The notion of "better" makes no sense unless it is underwritten by a particular view of what constitutes the good life. Rorty would have no quarrel with this, since he thinks that any conviction of what constitutes the good life is a community-supported notion. But this raises the question, which community? We live, after all, in a pluralistic world; most of us are able to identify with several different communities, with potentially competing visions of the good life. How does one choose among the competitors? A female academic of blue-collar roots in a liberal arts college, for example, could see herself as participating in the grand tradition of liberal education, as a woman seeking to reveal and supplant the oppression of patriarchal society, or as a grass-roots intellectual who wants to deflate the pretensions of academia. The things deemed "good in the way of belief" would be quite different in each case. How is she to adjudicate between the competing claims for her attention and commitments?[53]

The most appealing way to read Rorty is as though humans made up a species-specific community to which we can appeal, i.e., that there are certain truth claims, as well as certain value claims, that we "necessarily" assert in order to participate in the created human world in a meaningful way. Since the human species changes over time, these are not immutable truths, but merely the conditions necessary for the preservation and maintenance of a certain kind of life. On this basis, perhaps, one could construct suitable criteria for assessing the competing bids for attention in the previous example. Such a view appears to be one shared by Nietzsche (see above, Chapter Three) and has been developed with some degree of refinement by the sociologists of knowledge.[54]

While at times this seems to be Rorty's claim, in "Postmodernist Bourgeois Liberalism" he is quite critical of those who posit the existence of a "supercommunity—humanity as such" to justify particular historical claims to truth or value. In contrast he lauds those who believe "that there is no human dignity that is not derivative from the dignity of some specific community, and no appeal beyond the relative merits of various actual or proposed communities."[55]

What Rorty appears to be recommending, in other words, is the straightforward acceptance of the values and beliefs of the historical community to which one belongs. There is no "beyond" to which one can appeal to ground this community, no "way things are" that any particular community can or should reflect. There are simply the values, beliefs, and conditions of warranted assertability that comprise any particular community's meaning structure. The issue of competing claims from different communities is never addressed, nor are the boundaries and scope ever articulated for the nebulous "community" that is Rorty's constant refrain, nor finally is the radically pluralistic world many of us live ever taken seriously.[56]

Rorty acknowledges that his view prevents us from being able to say, for example, that our condemnation of the Holocaust is anything more than simply an expression of the distaste of one community. All we are saying, in other words, is that, "We don't do things like that." To the response from a community of National Socialists, "Well, *we* do," there is nothing more to be said. The difference is inadjudicable; all we can do is attempt to persuade (read: convert or coerce) people with different views to adopt our own.

As we have seen, at times Rorty speaks as though he regards this aspect of his thought as a defect, or at least, a problem worthy of attention, for it appears to have replaced the vocabulary of moral outrage with the vocabulary of the bigger gun. He writes, for example, that "this moral objection states the really important issue about textualism and pragmatism."[57] Yet at other times, he asserts quite unequivocally that the inability to criticize the practices of another group beyond appealing to the norms of one's own group can hardly be considered an objection. Speaking of Dewey and Gadamer, Rorty writes,

> Neither has any fulcrum outside the moral consensus embodied in our moral discourse to which they can appeal. Their only reply to this argument, therefore, is

> who *has* such a fulcrum? What would such a fulcrum look like? Who *can* give a 'rational refutation' of Hitler or Stalin? What could such a 'refutation' look like?[58]

Rorty's position is, otherwise stated, that "we should not regret our inability to perform a feat which no one has any idea of how to perform."[59]

Thus Rorty's stance on the question of nihilism mirrors the ambivalence seen in Miller's essay. He says, in effect, that anti-foundationalism is not nihilism, if by nihilism is meant the anarchism of Ivan Karamazov, "If God is dead, then everything is permitted." There are clear and, it appears to Rorty, unambiguous standards of what is and is not permitted by any given historical community, both ethically and epistemologically. If, however, by nihilism we mean that we cannot get out of our own skins, that we cannot transcend the particularities and contingencies of history, that there is no final truth about things, then, yes, for Rorty anti-foundationalism is nihilism—but there is nothing wrong with that. This is simply the way things are, and the way that they have always been. Rather than wringing our hands in mock-heroic despair, says Rorty, we should turn away from an issue which is, in the final analysis, just not that interesting, and get on with our lives.

Part III

The Resolution of Nihilism

6

Discontented versus Unrepentant Nihilists

In 1843 Soren Kierkegaard published a two-volume work called *Either/Or.* Although he distanced himself from its ideas through the use of an elaborate pseudonymous edifice (as would become typical of him), Kierkegaard's intent was to present to his readers two distinct types of people, and with them, two distinct categories of existence. His subsequent works further honed the different categories into a number of distinct types, but the basic distinction introduced in *Either/Or* remained fundamental.[1] We are presented with, on the one hand, the aesthetic mode; the aesthete defines himself and his life completely in terms of the temporal, finite, historical world—his principal goal is to maintain his interest and pleasure in his surroundings, his biggest fear is boredom. He believes in nothing more or larger than his own immediate sphere of influence. This is contrasted, on the other hand, with the ethical or the ethical-religious mode. The ethical-religious individual recognizes his temporal, finite, and historical nature, but places it in relation to something that transcends it, either the universal moral law (deemed absolutely binding) or God. As the title of the 1843 work indicates, the conjunction of the two is really an absolute *dis*junction—the two types of life are mutually exclusive.[2]

The distinction Kierkegaard made more than a century ago is a useful tool for characterizing the two post-Nietzschean responses to nihilism examined above. Barth's attempt to make nihilism the bearer of the Christian gospel can be seen as an instance of the ethical-religious, in which the historicity of the individual is at once affirmed and transcended; one seeks constantly to affirm one's relation to an absolute that, although invisible to human eyes and before which human reason is inarticulate, is paradoxically believed to be ultimately real and the only thing worthy of commitment. In contrast, Rorty recommends that "we try to get to the point where we no longer worship *anything*, where we treat *nothing* as a quasi-divinity, where we treat *everything*—our language, our conscience, our community—as a product of time and chance."[3] His almost indifferent acceptance of nihilism coupled with his apparent revelry over the intellectual controversies he creates reminds one of the aesthetic characters in volume 1 of *Either/Or.*[4]

Both the aesthetic and the ethical-religious responses to nihilism welcome it, in a sense, because both use nihilism as a means for criticizing the tradition that has come before them. Barth embraces epistemological nihilism as a polemic against religion, theology, and the absolute hubris of human beings in their attempts to reach God. All such attempts, in his eyes, come to nought, for no merely human knowledge can lead to truth. Rorty's alethiological nihilism leads him to dismiss the philosophical tradition since Descartes—but arguably going back to Plato—for its path down a blind alley, one which leads us only to frustration. Both Barth and Rorty, in other words, stand in the tradition of Nietzsche in that nihilism is in some sense a weapon used to reveal how hollow are the pretensions of human beings to be able to find truth. Both men employ some version of nihilism to uncover the problematic relationship between human beings and truth. Yet the difference between their views is far more striking than their similarities, and it is easily seen that Barth and Rorty are as absolutely disjoined as are the first and second volumes of *Either/Or.*

For Barth, nihilism is equivalent to the loss of humanly knowable absolutes; this loss was seen as something problematic, not to say terrifying, for it prompts a radical disorientation and chaos that throws everything into question. Human beings live in a world revealed to be devoid of purpose and meaning, of goodness and truth. This is nihilism in the mode of Ivan Karamazov; the loss of a readily apprehended ground or absolute authority makes the world one of random chaos that is terrifying in its arbitrariness. But Barth's appeal (either implicit or explicit) to an anthropological vision that sees this questionableness as an ethical or religious challenge—the call to be a certain kind of person in face of the nothingness that surrounds us—made the advent of nihilism, despite its terror, both tolerable and, in a sense, desirable. One could understand the chaos, the onslaught of meaninglessness, because it was not the sole or final word: There was a context in which the apparent arrival of meaninglessness was intelligible. Thus the appeal to transcendence, to some hidden but still real absolute remained; transmuted, yes, but nevertheless present, undergirding this outlook in a crucial way. God's absence became an indication of his presence, atheism a testimony to his power, and despair an essential component of faith.[5] Although Barth's early writings are in some ways much more obviously nihilistic than Rorty's—since Barth utterly denies the possibility of human knowledge, while Rorty believes that knowledge still exists[6]—they are nonetheless incompletely nihilistic; Barth's nihilism is *only* epistemological, not alethiological. There remains a wider context in which his nihilism is placed. Barth, in other words, still believes in Truth (i.e., God), even though there is no way this Truth can be known; our only relationship to it is by faith through grace.

Rorty's prose is missing the kind of romantic hysteria that much of Barth's writing borders on; the dense, often turgid, always flamboyant prose of *Romans* contrasts vividly with the clean and lucid prose that typifies Rorty's work. Rorty acknowledges that the world lacks any underlying ground or Author to which or to whom we can appeal for meaning and final justification. Thus, in one sense, Rorty is throwing in his lot with the Barthian view of nihilism, for he asserts, time and again, that no humanly knowable absolutes exist. But rather than regarding this with horror, or using the dissolution of humanly attainable truth as a springboard to faith, Rorty believes that this requires no closet appeal to transcendence, no larger framework in which it can be explained and interpreted, even in the limited way in which the theology of crisis explained it. Even stronger: Rorty regards (or appears to regard) such appeals as an instance of bad faith or of weakness. For Rorty, there simply isn't anything outside the humanly constructed systems of meaning to which we can appeal to resolve interpretive controversy. There are simply competing interpretations playing off one another; which one actually reigns is a function of the needs and interests of the bearers. While *within* a particular community (or, borrowing from Wittgenstein, "language game") there are rules governing our choice of beliefs—and hence, legitimate, justified belief (i.e., knowledge) is possible—there is no extrinsic criterion for choosing *between* communities (or language games): "Notions of criteria and choice (including that of 'arbitrary' choice) are no longer in point when it comes to changes from one language game to another" (*Contingency, Irony, and Solidarity*, 6). Such a decision is simply a matter of taste. Or, as he puts it, there is no meaningful distinction to be drawn between rational judgment and cultural bias.[7]

Rorty would be considered an epistemological nihilist, if by knowledge we meant justified true belief, because he frankly regards the notion of truth as, philosophically speaking, a dead end. But if we take his views on their own terms, we must redefine knowledge as simply justified belief—justified, that is, relative to the community to which we belong. And since Rorty does regard judgments about the legitimacy of beliefs as both possible and appropriate within these confines, to label him an epistemological nihilist is inaccurate. As we have seen, however, he is—or at least appears to be—an alethiological nihilist, for he rejects all conversation about truth as irrelevant. In his view the loss of truth should occasion no despair, for with it we lose nothing of any importance, since knowledge remains unchanged with its departure.[8]

Both Barth and Rorty attribute some stature to Nietzsche as a forerunner of their views—an interesting phenomenon, given the differences in their forms of nihilism. But it is not surprising, first, because Nietzsche has within him elements of both the aesthete and the religious thinker, and second, because the nature and extent of his nihilism(s) is a matter of no little debate.[9] Both Barth and Rorty, of course, see their inheritance of Nietzsche as partial; each, in effect, rejects that part of Nietzsche which leads to the position of the other. While recent scholarship has attended more to the aesthetic implications of Nietzsche's thought, pointing out the many connections between Nietzsche, Derrida, Rorty, and postmodern thought more generally, a number of scholars have read Nietzsche as primarily a religious thinker.[10] Which Nietzsche one finds depends, in part, on which elements of his thought one emphasizes.

One of the issues that divides Nietzsche scholars and is relevant here is his controversial stance on truth—did he or did he not think truth was possible? To what extent, and in what sense, did he think knowledge was possible? The aesthetic interpretation stresses his deconstruction of the notion of truth. This line would argue that Nietzsche was a *de facto* nihilist—certainly an alethiological nihilist, definitely an ethical nihilist, and probably an epistemological nihilist, depending on how one defines the terms. As I have argued above, however, there is a basic ambiguity—not to say ambivalence—in Nietzsche's analysis of nihilism. He seems both to welcome it and to view it as a crisis. This ambiguity makes assessing the state of nihilism within his thought difficult.

But it is at best imprecise, at worst inaccurate to see Nietzsche as an unambiguous champion of nihilism in any of its forms, for two reasons. First, he regarded nihilism as a destructive disease. To be sure, we can "return from such sickness...new born," but we can also perish. Nietzsche's goal was, finally, to overcome the decadence that was beginning to paralyze European culture (a decadence of which nihilism was the most obvious symptom.) Second, and perhaps more important, sustained nihilism would signal the demise of the necessarily interpretive character of human life.

While one might argue that Nietzsche viewed existential nihilism (the experience of meaninglessness) as the central problem facing European culture, but could—and did—embrace alethiological nihilism, this view cannot account for Nietzsche's sustained commitment to truthfulness, discussed in Chapter Three, pp. 44ff., above, nor his view that nihilism was a "respite" in the battle with truth. The interpretation given here reads him not as a nihilist, but takes at more or less face value his claim that he had "lived through the whole of nihilism, to the end, leaving it behind, outside himself" (WP: Preface, 4). Nietzsche dabbled in three forms of nihilism—epistemological, alethiological, and existential—but his philosophy is incoherent unless he did in fact leave at least the last two forms of it behind. Given the central place that the imposition of meaning plays in his anthropology, he could not sustain existential nihilism without contradiction, nor can he intelligibly be read as an alethiological nihilist, if nihilism is indeed a "respite" in the "battle" for truth.[11]

There is a sense, perhaps, in which he is a qualified epistemological nihilist, for he did redefine knowledge with his radical perspectivism; with this redefinition comes a radically new picture of human life. This perhaps helps to explain how both Rorty and Barth could find in him a friendly face. Rorty can appeal to Nietzsche's radically perspectival epistemology, his analysis of a culture's values and beliefs as an expression of (mostly unconscious) forces, while Barth could turn to the vision of transformed humanity built on the rubble of earlier religious and philosophical pretension, a vision that haunts so much of what Nietzsche wrote. Henri Bouillard writes,

> There is, in Barth as in Nietzsche, a desire to go beyond (*dépasser*) the excessively human sphere of religion, of morality, of culture, an obsession with the limit and the extreme, the pursuit of knowledge in non-knowledge and of the highest hope in the most profound distress, the same state of being torn between the abyss and the height.[12]

Where Nietzsche differs from both Barth and Rorty, however, is that he thought nihilism to be a temporary phenomenon, linked to a particular set of intellectual developments—the self-dissolution of the Platonic-Christian world view. In contrast, Barth and Rorty both regard nihilism as somehow endemic to the human process, something which, humanly speaking, cannot be changed or avoided. Even though Barth's nihilism is embedded in a wider context, the nihilism is not "left behind, outside oneself," as Nietzsche would have it; it remains an integral part of human life. Nor does Rorty think we will ever discover the missing ground or foundation, for no such entity exists. Thus one thing—and perhaps the only thing—that Barth and Rorty share is a de-historicized concept of nihilism. Nihilism is not the product of specifiable historical conditions, but something endemic to human life. The reasons each sees nihilism as intrinsic to human life, however, are quite different, and help to account for their different responses to nihilism.

Barth accepts the crisis value of nihilism, which was such a dominant theme in Nietzsche's analysis, as we have seen. This portrayal of nihilism as provoking some kind of existential crisis is crucial to his position, for this is what gives nihilism its salvific power. The confrontation with nihilism has the power to transform individuals because it throws into question the world in which they are unreflectively immersed. It makes them see what they are, and, more important, brings into relief all that they are not. Nihilism brings with it a higher truth, a truth that makes the experience of nihilism potentially transformative.

In Barth's eyes, nihilism is an expression of the distance between human beings and God, of human isolation from the divine; nihilism, in other words, is a function of sin. Full recognition of this, however, is possible only as a divinely generated gift. So great is human sin that we can only come to recognize it if God reveals our sinful nature to us. This is important for two reasons. First, the claim that the full-fledged experience of nihilism could only be of divine origin is Barth's sole defense against the conversion of his position into a negative natural theology. If nihilism identifies the human condition accurately, and if the experience of nihilism both tells us who we are and what God is, what need is there of divine grace or revelation? Cannot each individual, simply through contemplation on his or her own private wretchedness, come to genuine religious faith? Barth argued that one could not—only God can promote an awareness of nihilism in all of its depth, and with that, the possibility of faith. Not all of the dialectical theologians shared this antipathy toward natural theology, however, and this was one of the factors leading to its relatively quick demise and prompting Barth to move in other directions, seeking to purge his thought of the insidious influence of Kierkegaard and existentialism.

Second, since sin is present regardless of whether we see it or not (and indeed, our inability to see it is itself an expression of our sinful natures), this implies that nihilism is present whether we experience it or not. In other words, the connection of nihilism to human sinfulness makes nihilism a constant concomitant of the human situation, rather than a phenomenon linked to a particular set of historical occurrences.

In addition to the crisis overtones in his portrayal of nihilism, Barth also shared with Nietzsche a conviction of its fundamentally ambiguous nature. Nihilism is something both bad and good. The *condition* of nihilism is bad, in that it signals our distance from God, but the *experience* of nihilism is potentially good, since the recognition of our fallen and corrupt nature is the precondition of genuine religious faith. This experience brings with it an awareness of God and who he is—though an awareness, as we have seen, that is marked by its absence of cognitive content. "Through what they are not, men participate in who God is" (*Romans*, 121). Thus Barth shares with Nietzsche a sense for the crisis implicit in nihilism as well as a conviction about its ambiguous character. But by linking nihilism to human sinfulness, Barth made nihilism ahistorical, something that always characterizes human life "on this side of the resurrection." Nihilism becomes an inevitable feature of human life, whether we recognize it or not.

If this is the case, though—if nihilism is in fact inevitable—how can we object to it? Isn't it futile to protest something that is outside our power to change? Barth could (and did) appeal to the understanding of humanity found in the Bible: We *should* struggle against sin/nihilism because humans were originally created in a condition without sin. Nihilism is a consequence of the fall; it is inevitable, but not necessary. Thus a picture of human life in the absence of nihilism implicitly underwrites Barth's protest against it. In the absence of such a picture, however, protesting something inevitable seems futile. From this point it is only a short step to the claim that protesting nihilism is not only futile, but silly.

Rorty takes this short step, apparently without looking back. We cannot condemn ourselves for not being able to do something that no one knows how to do and that no one has ever been able to do. God is not dead—he never existed in the first place. The only thing we lose with the acknowledgement of nihilism is the compulsion to fulfil a standard beyond our reach. With Rorty, in other words, nihilism has moved from being the experience of the loss of absolutes (Nietzsche) to the simple fact that there are no absolutes. This fact is not one that generates a crisis, but relieves us of a responsibility that was always impossible to fulfill. Properly understood, nihilism means not the loss of absolutes (for this implies that such absolutes once existed), but the loss of the command to live up to absolutes we now recognize do not exist. Since this is a loss from which we all benefit, we should recognize nihilism as an unambiguously good thing.

If we can speak for a moment of a kind of historical progression from Nietzsche, through Barth, to Rorty, we see a subtle but important shift in the understanding of nihilism: nihilism has been transformed from a means of liberation to something intrinsically liberating. Nietzsche regarded nihilism as an inevitable but temporary stage in human development. Its temporary nature was necessary, for to embrace nihilism as the final word would lead, in his eyes, to death. He also saw it as a stage linked to particular and specifiable historical developments: the unfolding of the Platonic-Christian tradition. For all of the dangers he associated with it, he nonetheless believed that it could serve as a spur to create healthier, more affirmative forms of life. Thus Nietzsche believed nihilism to be a weapon or a tool used to improve the current state.

Similarly, Barth's engagement with nihilism was colored by his conviction that this state of dissolution and despair was revelatory of something fundamental and other than nihilism: It revealed to us who and what we are. Thus the appraisal of nihilism was grounded in a certain vision of human nature, one which saw the self as defined by, literally, nothing, as existing in the tension created between oppositions, in the conflict between sin and faith, between inauthenticity and authenticity. This view of the self sought to replace the sure possession of objective truth (something deemed in this view as impossible for humans to possess) with the ongoing search for subjective truthfulness; in Barth's word, with "faith." Thus, while human knowledge leads only to untruth and error, the conflict that this realization was seen to engender reflected a deeper commitment to an ideal of truthfulness which made the experience of nihilism tolerable. Precisely this commitment to something more enabled the dialectical theologians to wrest salvific power from something initially experienced as paralyzing and inescapable.

Rorty, however, makes no appeal to some higher truth. For him, nihilism is simply the expression of the fact that "nothing grounds our practices, nothing legitimizes them, nothing shows them to be in touch with the way things are";[13] it is a reflection of our "inability to get out of our own skins." And for Rorty this common-sense observation promotes relief, if it promotes anything at all. Thus the shift away from the ethical-religious response—which attempts to wrest from nihilism some kind of salvific power—to the aesthetic response is likewise a shift away from the terror and the anxiety nihilism provoked in the earlier part of its history to rather calm acceptance, if not outright relief. Existential nihilism has dropped out of the picture.

The dissolution or absence of existential nihilism is, of course, not the only difference between the views of Barth and of Rorty. As I have already discussed, Barth's nihilism was epistemological, Rorty's is alethiological. Barth, that is, rejected knowledge but believed in truth, while Rorty rejects truth but believes that knowledge still is possible. This difference helps to explain, perhaps, how existential nihilism—in the nineteenth century, an almost automatic inference from other forms of nihilism—could disappear. Only if we are unconvinced or reluctant nihilists would nihilism provoke anxiety or discomfort; only if we still believe in truth can our isolation from it provoke discomfort. The pathos that Nietzsche described—the world is not what we thought it was—

implies a conflict or a disparity between what the world appears to be and what we want it to be. To be undisturbed by the loss of truth implies that we no longer compare what the world is like to what we want or hope it to be like, what we think it should be like. Existential nihilism, in other words, can only take root if the other forms of nihilism are incomplete or partial.

This suggests that the aesthetic response to nihilism is to embrace it wholeheartedly. The anti-foundationalists view the absence of truth calmly—as opposed to their nineteenth- and early twentieth-century forebears—because their nihilism is complete. Since there is and could be nothing larger than the discrete historical world in which we live, since the very notion of something larger (it is held) lapses into incoherence as soon as one tries to articulate what that something is, there is nothing to compare our present reality with; consequently, there is no impetus or basis for any feeling of dissatisfaction or despair.

This shift from the ethical-religious to the aesthetic shows how much the interpretation of nihilism has changed since Nietzsche first proclaimed its unfolding to be "the history of the next two centuries."[14] Nineteenth-century thinkers generally saw nihilism as situated in a particular historical time—their own—linking it to the erosion of external bases of authority and the tyranny of individual consciousness, fostered by Romantic subjectivity, on the one hand, and Enlightenment rationalism, on the other. Nietzsche both deepened this historical thesis and sublated it at the same time. On the one hand, he linked nihilism to a particular historical event: the self-dissolution of the Platonic-Christian world view. On the other hand, his philosophical perspectivism served to de-historicize nihilism by making it appear to be simply an expression of the multiplicity of possible interpretations of the world. The dialectical theologians mimicked this tension between the historical and the ahistorical interpretations of nihilism, asserting, on the one hand, that they lived in a privileged age, in that the problem of nihilism had come to the fore then as it had in no other, on the other hand arguing that it was nonetheless universal and ahistorical in that it was the secular counterpart to sin. The anti-foundationalists complete the ahistoricizing process, in effect, by completely removing the historical overtones to nihilism, simultaneously taking the sting out of sin. What was anathema to many in the nineteenth century—the multiplicity of interpretations—becomes for some, in the late twentieth century, an occasion for "joyous affirmation."

I do not wish to imply that this was a simple and straightforward linear progression—this would require me to make claims of historical influence at best difficult to prove—nor am I claiming that we are all anti-foundationalists and/or unrepentant nihilists; the sheer controversy surrounding the advent of postmodernism, if nothing else, belies the latter. But if a pattern emerges from the studies in this volume, it suggests that the last century has seen the gradual dissolution of the pathos of nihilism—a dissolution abetted by the existentialist appropriation of it as revelatory of the character of human existence itself—into the bathos of nihilism in the contemporary scene. Nihilism is, at least for some people, a matter of no concern, as starkly evident in Cornel West's blithe pronouncement that "the shock effect of Catastrophic nihilism is now boring and uninteresting."[15]

I have tried to show that a shift, at least in some circles, has taken place away from the nineteenth-century view that nihilism is something problematic and troublesome to the view that nihilism is, in three short words, no big deal. In the remainder of this chapter I want to explore some of the consequences of this transformation. What do we gain when we find nihilism banal? What do we lose? How should those of us who are not yet unrepentant nihilists view this turn of events?

If Rorty is correct, what we gain is considerable. We lose the compulsion to live up to standards impossible to fulfill; we quit berating ourselves for failing to discover a "rational refutation of Hitler," or of child abuse, or of the torture of innocents. Since no such refutation could exist, our inability to discover it should occasion no guilt or grief—instead, we should simply give up the attempt. We ought frankly and unabashedly to accept the "post-modern bourgeois liberal" society in which we live as our way, and therefore a way that is good and right. No justification beyond this appeal to our own practice is necessary because none is possible. Happily, since toleration, pluralism, and freedom of expression are part of this community, we gain all of that too. The fanaticism of earlier eras and other cultures is not part of our view.

Thus described, the implications of a domesticated form of nihilism seem quite positive. Yet a growing number of commentators on Rorty's writings are less sanguine about its consequences, querying whether anti-foundationalism, as Rorty presents it, finally has the beneficent consequences just described. In particular, a number of critics are concerned about the latent conservatism of Rorty's position, charging that his defense of liberalism and the free exchange of ideas is really a simple justification of the status quo.

Thomas McCarthy, for example, examines the separation between politics and philosophy that Rorty enjoins. On Rorty's model, we should not seek to show that liberalism is most conducive to the flourishing of human nature, or that it is morally the superior form of government, because all such attempts reflect a belief in transcendent truths that simply do not exist. There is, finally, no such thing as "human nature" or "the morally superior form of government"; there are simply the ways certain communities view themselves and their societies. We should, therefore, unabashedly affirm our practice and beliefs without worrying about the demand by (old-fashioned) foundationalists that we justify or account for them. In McCarthy's mind, the upshot of this is quite damning:

> Critical thought is aestheticized and privatized, stripped of any social-political implications. There can be no politi-

> cally relevant critical theory and hence no theoretically informed critical practice.... We are prevented from even thinking, in any theoretically informed way, the thought that the basic structures of society might be inherently unjust in some way that they might work to the systematic disadvantage of certain social groups.[16]

To assess and evaluate the particular social milieu in which we find ourselves, McCarthy argues, requires "transcultural notions of validity" (361). Rorty is guilty of "the 'God is dead, everything is permitted' fallacy of disappointed expectations" (361); his response to the recognition of the historical and bounded nature of human knowledge is "a pendulum swing to...anti-rationalist extremes." A more appropriate and helpful response, in McCarthy's eyes, is to try "to develop concepts of reason, truth, and justice that, while no longer pretending to a God's-eye point of view, retain something of their transcendent, regulative, critical force" (367), something he sees being done in work of Hilary Putnam and Juergen Habermas.

Richard Bernstein has also suggested that the "'aestheticised pragmatism' that Rorty advocates...begins to look...[like] little more than an *apologia* for the status quo."[17] Rorty has, in effect, substituted a"'historical myth of the given' for the 'epistemological myth of the given' that he has helped to expose" (551). In consequence, he treats complex and multifaceted phenomena like "liberalism" as though they were simple and unambiguous, comprising only one community, all in happy agreement, or at least tolerant of (which Bernstein reads as "indifferent to") disagreement, a problem we have already discussed briefly just above (pp. 113ff.). Bernstein writes,

> [Rorty] tends to gloss over what appears to be the overwhelming "fact" of contemporary life—the breakdown of moral and political consensus, and the conflicts and incompatibility among competing social practices. Even if Rorty thinks that claims about the breakdown of moral and political consensus are exaggerated, one would expect

> some *argument* showing why the 'crisis mentality' of the twentieth century is mistaken—or at least a clarification of what are the characteristics of the consensus that he thinks does exist among those who take themselves to be champions of liberal democracy. It is never clear why Rorty, who claims that there is no consensus about competing conceptions of the good life, thinks there is any more consensus about conceptions of justice or liberal democracy. (552)

What Bernstein finds "most objectionable" about Rorty's position is that "it diverts us from the pragmatically important issues that need to be confronted" (546)—for example, who are the "we" that Rorty constantly invokes.

The result of Rorty's aversion to theory, in other words, seems to lead to the perpetuation of the present structures of society. Both Bernstein and McCarthy argue that Rorty's anti-foundationalism not only serves to reinforce the dominant social beliefs and practices of our culture, but also undercuts any possible social criticism. All we need, Rorty says, are the beliefs and practices of our community; since they are all we have, there is, it would seem, no basis on which to assess them. Any attempt to do so is dismissed as the bad-faith effort to adopt a God's-eye view.[18]

What this suggests is that the banalization of nihilism ultimately culminates in nihilism's opposite: dogmatism—the unrelenting insistence upon one's own position, one's own point of view, immune to any sort of criticism or rational scrutiny. When we fully and happily dispatch with truth, what we gain is not pluralism, not toleration, but rather the absolutization of the dominant power structures of the culture to which we belong. Nihilism, once complete, leaves us with nothing but the set of currently existing social practices and beliefs; in the absence of anything else, these practices and beliefs become, for all intents and purpose, absolute.

By his own admission, Rorty is concerned about the threat of dogmatism, and seems to recognize some of the dangers of his own position, as we have discussed above.

In *Philosophy and the Mirror of Nature*, he lauds the edifying philosophers for their continual attempts to uncover and expose dogmatism. Edifying philosophers help keep us intellectually honest; they remind us of the partial and limited perspective that any human being has. Rorty also recognizes the need, as he puts it, for each individual to have "more than one intellectual hero"; one hero to a customer breeds fanaticism. To remind us of our own "fallibilism," it is necessary that we be able to criticize our own points of view. "What enables us to make such criticisms," he writes "is concrete alternative suggestions—suggestions about how to redescribe what we are talking about."[19] McCarthy's notion of truth as a regulative idea is ultimately "empty and powerless" because these concrete alternative suggestions are sufficient in themselves to give us critical leverage (635).

We can agree with Rorty that one thing that can help immunize us from dogmatism is sheer exposure to a variety of possible perspectives, but we cannot stop there. Unless we believe that there is some way to adjudicate between competing suggestions, we have no way of choosing between them; as a result, either we will regard them all as equally valid (or invalid), or we will privilege our own to the exclusion of others. In a sense, of course, this latter course of action is what Rorty wants, since this is what ethnocentrism finally means. What he wants to avoid, however, is making our own community's views absolute. Rorty suggests that simply knowing about other points of view, having them presented in an attractive and compelling way, will keep us intellectually humble and also enable us to criticize and assess our own points of view.

But how would it do that, if I recognize, with Rorty, that rational judgment is simply another way of saying "cultural bias" and that my truths are simply my tastes? If indeed there are no criteria that enable us to judge between language games, it is not clear how knowing of the existence of other games helps me gain critical leverage on my own. Only if I can compare the two and find my own wanting, would such juxtaposition prove useful. I might, perhaps, "convert" to the new language game, but while this might relativize my old perspective, it would simply transfer my absolutized allegiance somewhere new.

Rorty might say that I have missed the point; he is not asking us to relinquish our beliefs, only to recognize their limited and finite nature. We are free to continue to hold them, but exposure to other, competing beliefs will simply serve to temper our enthusiasm, will rein in our sense of commitment. The ethnocentrism he advocates need not culminate in absolutism, for the confrontation with opposing views will keep us from generalizing our community's beliefs into universal truths.

Or will it? The progression from pluralism to fallibilism is not at all transparent. Confronting opposing views—or even views that are simply different—can just as easily lead me to cling all the more strongly to the beliefs I hold. If, however, this confrontation leads me to regard competing claims about the same matter simply as the expression of different ways of doing things, won't I conclude that the competing claims are all essentially equal? Won't, in other words, it result in a subjectivistic leveling of knowledge into mere opinion? If all of our knowledge claims—claims that are well justified within our particular community, but with no support beyond that—are matters of subjective preference (like, perhaps, an aversion to lima beans), then it seems that we have not moved beyond vulgar relativism after all. Either I generalize my (private) tastes into universal truths—the essence of absolutism—or I recognize them simply as my private tastes, with no more nor less substance to them than the opinions of others. In either case, the result seems far removed from the ethnocentrism that Rorty thinks is healthy and appropriate. We seem, in other words, to be caught in the very impasse Rorty tacitly rejects: Either we dogmatically assert our views to be the only views possible or we believe only that our views are essentially on par with those of everyone else and we are thus awash in a relativistic morass. Both results destroy any possible leverage for criticism.[20]

This argument can be restated more clearly, perhaps, in terms of the discussion in the preceding chapters. One of the lessons we learn from Rorty is that resistance to nihilism shows our commitment to standards that nihilism itself undermines, a lesson we also learned with Nietzsche. The very intellectual tradition we have revered leads to its own destruction; as Rorty has said, our concern about its destruction shows our continuing commitment to intellectual intuitions that are outmoded and passé. It is because of our expectations of truth that we feel the absence of truth as a problem. Rorty's solution to this problem is to jettison the notion of truth. But Nietzsche's version of this same lesson had a second part to it: that nihilism, while inevitable, and necessary, and itself a state of tension, must be temporary—either we give birth to new ways of valuing, new forms of believing, or we perish. The will to interpret, to impose our truths on our surroundings, is simply too strong.

Rorty, of course, does not wish to stop interpreting, so it seems there is no problem. Barth, however, also has a lesson for us: In the absence of something higher, something larger than themselves, some transcendent horizon, human beings make themselves God. And a sense that there is something more, something higher to which we must be responsible, something more to life than what we have captured and understood, is essential to avoid this. We cannot recognize the limited and relative nature of our own points of view without some sense of the coherence of a non-relative point of view. Unless we believe that there is more to the world than that revealed to us by currently existing human discourse and activity, we will believe that the currently existing human discourse and activity is all that there is. Existing beliefs and practices, in other words, will completely fill the horizon, becoming the sole, in effect, the absolute, reality. When we deny the existence of truth, we are left only with the status quo, and the status quo will then acquire the status of truth.

The aesthetic revaluation of nihilism makes truth a matter of taste, of individual and cultural preferences. Religious and ethical questions are reinterpreted to be matters of personal choice, for there exist no criteria beyond private decision by which to evaluate them. It may appear that such a move promotes toleration, for it implies that, just as few people would argue to the death about the merits of Springsteen versus Dylan, so too should we not argue violently about the existence or non-existence of God, or the superiority of Confucianism over Christianity. Civilized disputes, to be sure, are welcome, operating within the boundaries of what a well-educated person deems acceptable, but we should not expect or seek to find final resolution in such matters, for we have no access to a criterion that would provide such resolution.[21]

Undergirding this air of bemused toleration, however, is a dogmatism that belies its apparent openmindedness, a dogmatism of the most frightening kind. The aestheticization of preference—the making of moral and religious choice a matter of community taste with no justification beyond the banal remark, "But we've always done it this way"—removes all possibility of justification and therefore all need to be responsible and self-aware in one's decisions and commitments, beyond one's participation in the particular community of which one is a member. Since no justification is possible, none can be required. One is left with simply the blind assertion of one's private will; if the particular community to which one belongs does not support one's will, one simply finds (or creates) a community more sympathetic to one's tastes.

This dogmatism is linked to the lack of any sense of concern over the absence of some standard to which we can appeal. The sense of crisis that the loss of God engendered as described by the dialectical theologians did more than sanctify misery by providing it with meaning—it also provided the space and leverage necessary for any kind of criticism and any kind of self-conscious, self-directed change. The gap between what is and what we hope for is what motivates us to try to change our present surroundings and prevents us from succumbing to the all-too-pervasive power of inertia. The conviction—or at least, the hope—that we are not all that we can be is the fuel that keeps us going in situations that seem to thwart any positive change.

Similarly, the ability to distinguish between the norms and beliefs of the particular community to which we belong and what has more generally been called "the Good" and "the True" is an essential aspect of any cultural criticism. It was this ability that led Barth to be a leader in the Confessing Church, a movement that resisted Hitler's demand for absolute allegiance. In response to Hitler's demand, Barth asserted that nothing in this world can legitimately demand absolute allegiance, for nothing in this world is absolute. Only God merits such allegiance. Consistently applied, Barth's position offered a fail-safe protection against fanaticism, for there is nothing humanly knowable worthy of such absolute devotion. The commitment to an unknown God serves as a check, in other words, ensuring that no human belief is ever elevated to the status of the highest truth. Rorty's position, however, offers no such protection; his view is in fact an unabashed affirmation of a particular way of life—"ours," says Rorty, which finally, it seems, means no more than "his"—to the exclusion of all others. The only thing his view can be criticized for, he says, is excessive commitment to the particular community of which one is a member.

An "excessive commitment to a particular community," however, is no small thing. History bears sufficient examples, some in quite recent memory, where such commitment has had horrendous consequence; it is not something about which we can afford to be sanguine. But it appears to be an inevitable consequence of the full-fledged adoption of alethiological nihilism for, unlike his existentialist predecessors, Rorty has lost the critical edge afforded by the refusal to view nihilism as the final word. The ultimate result of this is making the trivial absolute, for there is nothing to prevent identifying our particular truths and values with "the Truth." In the absence of some kind of commitment to something greater than the community, however nebulous and ill-formed the object of this commitment be, the community itself becomes absolute. At its least offensive, this fosters a kind of smugness commented on even by one of Rorty's more adamant supporters.[22] At its worst, it fosters a blind dogmatism that neither knows nor can know any limits. When one accepts nihilism as "just the way things are," it ceases to be a potential weapon against corrupt and decaying modes of thought, as both Nietzsche and Barth employed it, and as Rorty says he too is employing it. The possibility of any kind of ethical, religious, or political transformation is *de facto* ruled out and the perpetuation of the status quo is covertly promoted. Any disagreements that do exist deteriorate, ultimately, into contests of power. The ultimate implications, in other words, of banalizing nihilism are anything but banal.

CONCLUSION

Nihilism, the bane of the nineteenth century, is fast becoming the banality of the late twentieth century. The loss of truth prophesied by Nietzsche has become reality in postmodern circles, yet without the attendant loss of meaning he also predicted. In the postmodern world, we can have meaning without truth because we can have knowledge without truth. The nineteenth-century belief that if truth disappeared, so too must knowledge and meaning, has been supplanted; in a world without truth (it is held) both knowledge and meaning still abound.

Nietzsche, of course, helped initiate the rift between knowledge and truth one finds both in Barth and in Rorty. His frequent dicta that our knowledge is really ignorance, our truths are lies, and our moral convictions are veiled assertions of power helped provoke the recognition of the allegedly empty character of our beliefs and the inveterately false nature of our knowledge. After Nietzsche, no unproblematic relation between knowledge and truth is possible—it seems, in fact, that no relation is possible at all. Both Barth and Rorty start from this point. Each severs completely the connection between knowledge and truth, but where one of them opts for truth, the other opts for knowledge. Both positions are marked by a certain pathos—either one has the truth but can never know it, or one has knowledge that bears no relation to truth. But only the former recognizes its pathos—Barth responds with despair to a world where true belief is never justified belief, in which justified beliefs are never true. Rorty by contrast responds with equanimity.

If one must choose between these two extremes, my own view is that truth without knowledge is preferable to knowledge without truth. Faith that is empty, devoid of any epistemic content, is, if nothing else, less dangerous than "knowledge" that is full of conviction and empty of truth. Although we tend to associate dogmatism with religious absolutism, in the present case, at least, the association is miscast. Here it is precisely religious absolutism in the Barthian sense that is the antidote for dogmatism. Barth's unrelenting insistence that "God is he whom we do not know" (*Romans,* 45) prevents the absolutization of any claim to knowledge. In contrast, Rorty's continual rejection of any need to justify or defend (in any non–self-referential way) the appropriateness of our current practices and beliefs leads to their sanctification.

Most of us cannot or will not return to the unabashedly blind faith of the dialectical theologians in a radically transcendent other, but we are equally uneasy simply to affirm the beliefs and practices that currently define liberal bourgeois culture. Fortunately, we need not choose between these two extremes, because there are alternatives; perhaps the most valuable lesson this volume has to offer is the importance of examining these alternatives with some care. Juergen Habermas' theory of communicative action is one attempt to strike a balance between the realities of historicism, of the finite, bounded nature of human discourse, and the demand that we relate ourselves to something larger than the discrete historical community to which we belong.[23] In quite a different vein, Donald Davidson shares with Rorty a critique of the correspondence theory of truth but is not, on that account, finished with truth. His recent lectures at Columbia University attempt to articulate a position that avoids the pitfalls of the correspondence view without forsaking the concept of truth.[24] Within religious studies, a number of thinkers are trying to theologize "deconstructively," creating a tradition of postmodern religious thought.[25] Dissimilar in kind those these attempts may be, the spirit behind them all is broadly the same: to admit the presence of Nietzsche's uncanniest of all guests without conceding to its power.

Notes

CHAPTER 1: THE PROBLEM OF NIHILISM

1. *Der Roemerbrief*, first edition 1919; second edition 1922. All quotations are from his *Epistle to the Romans*, trans. Edwyn Hoskyns (London, 1933; rpt. New York: Oxford University Press, 1977). This is a translation of the sixth edition, which is a reprint of the second edition. All further references to this work appear in the text.

2. Karl Adams, in *Hochland* (June 1926), quoted by John McConnachie, "The Teaching of Karl Barth: A New Positive Movement in German Theology," *Hibbert Journal*, 25 (1927), pp. 385–6.

3. Dialectical theology is known by a number of different names, including the "theology of crisis," "Barthianism," "neo-orthodox theology," and the "Theology of the Word of God." For the sake of simplicity I will restrict myself to "dialectical theology" or, occasionally, the "theology of crisis."

4. The problems defining existentialism are notorious, as most of the thinkers labelled "existentialists" accept the designation reluctantly, if at all. Nonetheless, sufficient similarities exist between Heidegger, Sartre, Camus, and Jaspers to warrant a common, if cautious, designation. For a useful account of the principal characteristics of existential thought (both theistic and non-theistic), see John Mac-

quarrie, "Existentialism," *The Encyclopedia of Religion*, ed. Mircea Eliade et al. (New York: Macmillan, 1986).

5. Friedrich Gogarten, "The Crisis of Our Culture," in *The Beginnings of Dialectical Theology*, vol. 1, trans. James M. Robinson (Richmond, Va.: John Knox Press, 1968), p. 295.

6. See Martin Heidegger, *Sein und Zeit*, especially section 40 (English translation by Edward Robinson and John Macquarrie, *Being and Time*, New York: Harper and Row, 1962), and Albert Camus, *The Myth of Sisyphus and Other Essays*, trans. Justin O'Brien (New York: Vintage Books, 1955).

7. See Otto Poegeller, "Hegel und die Anfaenge der Nihilismus-Diskussion," in *Der Nihilismus als Phaenomen der Geistesgeshichte in der wissenchaftlichen Diskussion unseres Jahrhundert*, ed. Dieter Arendt (Darmstadt: Wissenschaftliche Buchgesellschaft, 1974) and W. Goerdt, "Nihilismus," in *Historisches Woerterbuch der Philosophie*, ed. Joachim Ritter and Karlfried Gruender (Darmstadt: Wissenchaftliche Buchgesellschaft, 1984) for a discussion of the earliest uses of the term. See also Chapter Two, below.

8. Nietzsche, *Saemtliche Werke. Kritische Studienausgabe in 15 Baenden*, ed. Giorgio Colli and Mazzino Montinari (Munich: Deutscher Taschenbuch Verlag, 1980), vol. 13: part 11 [fragment 119]. All further references to this work appear in the text as KSA, followed by the volume, part, and (in brackets) fragment numbers. Where available, English translations are also cited. The selections from Nietzsche's notebooks that appear in *The Will to Power*, trans. Walter Kaufmann and R. J. Hollingdale (New York: Vintage Books, 1968) are cited as WP, followed by fragment number. I have quoted from the cited translations when listed; all other translations from the German are my own. All emphases in the quotations are in the original.

9. There has been surprisingly little attention paid to Nietzsche's influence on theology. The only thorough treatment of this issue is found in Peter Koester, "Nietzsche-Kritik und Nietzsche-Rezeption in der Theologie des 20. Jahrhundert," *Nietzsche Studien* 10/11 (1981/2), pp. 615–85. (For a discussion of Nietzsche's influence on "alternative religions," see Steven E. Aschheim, "After the Death of God: Varieties of Nietzschean Religion," *Nietzsche Studien* 17

(1988), pp. 218–49.) Nietzsche influenced the dialectical theologians both directly and indirectly: directly, in that members of this circle read Nietzsche's work and described him as one of their teachers; indirectly, through Nietzsche's more widespread influence on the apocalyptic self-consciousness of early-twentieth-century Germany.

10. Nicely captured in his pronouncement, "What a theologian takes to be true *must* be false; one has therein almost a criterion of truth" (*Der Antichrist*, paragraph 9: KSA 6, p. 175). Presumably Nietzsche's lifelong friend and confidant, Franz Overbeck, was exempted from this indictment.

11. I say this despite the frequently discussed parallels between Nietzsche's thought and postmodernism. As I will discuss below, on my reading of Nietzsche he has less in common with postmodernists than is generally assumed. See especially Chapter Six, pp. 123ff.

12. Jacques Derrida, *Of Grammatology*, trans. Gayatri Chakravorty Spivak (Baltimore: Johns Hopkins University Press, 1976), p. 158; Richard Rorty, *Consequences of Pragmatism* (Minneapolis: University of Minnesota Press, 1982), pp. xlii–xliii.

13. Jacques Derrida, "Tympan," in *Margins of Philosophy*, trans. Alan Bass (Chicago: University of Chicago Press, 1982), p. xii; for a sample of Rorty's denial, see his "Pragmatism, Relativism, and Irrationalism," in *Consequences of Pragmatism*, pp. 160–75.

14. The caveat "perhaps" is necessary, for Derrida's views on this issue are ambiguous. See below, Chapter Five, pp. 99ff.

15. This justification is probably all the more necessary since I suspect that those readers most familiar with Rorty know little of Barth, and vice versa. On the parallels between Nietzsche and Rorty see, for example, Daniel Shaw, "Rorty and Nietzsche: Some Elective Affinities" in *International Studies in Philosophy* 21:2 (1989), pp. 3–14. On Nietzsche and Barth, see Henri Bouillard, *Genèse et évolution de la théologie dialectique*, vol. I of *Karl Barth*. (Paris: Aubier, 1957).

16. These terms are borrowed from Soren Kierkegaard, and are

meant in roughly his sense. For a full account of their use here, see Chapter Six.

17. Their conjunction is also useful because I wish to argue against (or at least supplement) a commonly held view that Nietzsche and Rorty have much in common. On my reading of Nietzsche, he has more in common with Barth than with Rorty. Nietzsche, in other words, is more of a religious visionary than a playful aesthete (or, at the very least, he is as much of a visionary as an aesthete). This is seen nowhere more clearly than in his diagnosis of and response to nihilism.

18. Discussions of nihilism in English are usually limited to its treatment by Nietzsche or by Heidegger. (See, for example, David Michael Levin's *The Opening of Vision: Nihilism and the Postmodern Situation* [New York: Routledge & Kegan Paul, 1988]). While valuable, such discussions do not satisfy the need for a larger picture. Stanley Rosen's *Nihilism: A Philosophical Essay* (New Haven: Yale University Press, 1969), Alasdair MacIntyre's *After Virtue* (Notre Dame, Ind.: University of Notre Dame Press, 1981), and Allan Bloom's *The Closing of the American Mind* (New York: Simon and Schuster, 1987) are prominent (and typical) examples of works that discuss the problem of nihilism, but with a clear polemical intent in mind.

    Joseph Goudsblom's *Nihilism and Culture* (Totowa, New Jersey: Rowman and Littlefield, 1980) is less polemical than the latter works without sacrificing breadth of vision, but the work was written in the late 1950s (reprinted in an English translation) and thus predates the advent of movements like deconstruction. This leads Goudsblom to claim that the defining trait of twentieth-century nihilism is the desire to overcome it; as we shall see, this is not the case. Donald A. Crosby's recent book, *The Specter of the Absurd* (Albany: State University of New York Press, 1988), offers a comprehensive and helpful overview of what he labels "existential" nihilism; here too, however, nihilism is treated as an unambiguously undesirable state of mind.

    While there is a wide body of German scholarship on nihilism, the focus is primarily on either the analyses of Nietzsche and Heidegger or on the origins of the so-called nihilism debate among the German idealists.

CHAPTER 2: UNDERSTANDING NIHILISM

1. from the *Oxford English Dictionary*, 2nd ed., prepared by J. A. Simpson and E. S. C. Weiner (Oxford: Clarendon Press, 1989). Other related (although less common) words include "nihilianism," or the doctrine that the nature of Christ was only divine, containing no human element (also, by the way, one of the possible but archaic definitions of nihilism) and "nihility," the quality or state of being nothing.
2. Rosen, *Nihilism*, p. xiv.
3. See Poeggeler, "Hegel und die Anfaenge der Nihilismus-Diskussion."
4. Goudsblom locates an earlier, more casual usage in France (about the time of the French Revolution) to refer to "'one who is politically impartial'" or "'one who does not believe in anything'." See *Nihilism and Culture*, p. 3.
5. in Friedrich Jacobi, *Werke*, ed. Friedrich Roth and Friedrich Koeppen (Darmstadt: Wissenschaftliche Buchgesellschaft, 1968), pp. 3–57.
6. According to Goerdt ("Nihilismus," in *Historisches Woerterbuch des Philosophie*), Friedrich Koeppen extended Jacobi's criticism of Fichte to Schelling in *Schellings Lehre oder das Ganze der Philosophie des absoluten Nichts*, first published in 1803. In 1828 W. T. Krug further extended the link between idealism and nihilism by arguing that idealists must begin with nihilism, and then find that they are incapable of getting out of it; see his *Allgemein Handwoerterbuch des philosophische Wissenschaft*.
7. *Faith and Knowledge*, trans. Walter Cerf and H. S. Harris (Albany: State University of New York Press, 1977), p. 190.
8. Poeggeler, p. 320.
9. Jean Paul, "Poetische Nihilisten," in *Werke*, (Munich: Carl Hanser Verlag, 1963), pp. 459–60.
10. Even Hegel distinguished between good and bad forms of nihilism, and thought that to get mired in nihilism was a problem: the point was to wrest the Absolute from the absolute nothing. The only possible supporter of nihilism

during this period was a left-wing Hegelian, Max Stirner (a pseudonym for Johann Kaspar Schmidt). Stirner offered a view that seemed to embrace everything denounced as nihilistic by these critics. He never, however, explicitly described himself as a nihilist, which perhaps suggests that he also saw the term negatively.

11. *Fathers and Sons*, trans. Rosemary Edmonds (New York: Penguin, 1986) p. 94. Note the similarity between this characterization of nihilism and the description of enlightenment given by Kant in his essay "What is Enlightenment?":

> Enlightenment is man's release from his self-incurred tutelage. Tutelage is man's inability to make use of his understanding without direction from another. Self-incurred is this tutelage when its cause lies not in lack of reason but in lack of resolution and courage to use it without direction from another. *Sapere aude!* "Have courage to use your own reason!"—that is the motto of enlightenment. (Quoted from *Critique of Practical Reason and Other Writings in Moral Philosophy*, trans. Lewis White Beck [Chicago: University of Chicago, 1949], p. 286.)

This parallel suggests that the emergence of the term "nihilism" during the Enlightenment was no accident.

12. Given their crudely materialistic epistemology, however, the Russian nihilists are, from one point of view, at the opposite extreme from nihilism, despite their self-attribution. See Note 29 below.

13. Turgenev's own attitude toward the nihilism he characterized was probably more ambivalent. See Isaiah Berlin, "Fathers and Children" in the Edmonds translation of *Fathers and Sons*, pp. 7–61.

14. This is one of the reasons I have not included him in the present study, although both Rorty and Rudolf Bultmann (one of Barth's cohort) stand within the circle of his influence. Another reason is that Heidegger is already well represented in the secondary literature on nihilism. See Chapter One, Note 22.

15. Ernst Juenger, *Ueber die Linie* (Frankfurt: Vittorio Klostermann, 1950), p. 11.

16. in Rosen, *Nihilism,* p. 19.
17. Helmut Thielecke, *Nihilism: Its Origin and Nature, with a Christian Answer,* trans. John W. Doberstein (New York: Schocken Books, 1969), p. 115.
18. Karl Loewith, "The European Background of Contemporary Nihilism," in *Nature, History and Existentialism,* ed. Arnold Levinson (Evanston, Ill.: Northwestern University Press, 1966), p. 10.
19. Charles Glicksberg, *The Literature of Nihilism* (Lewisburg, Pa.: Bucknell University Press, 1975), p.13.
20. Albert Camus, *The Rebel,* trans. Anthony Bower (New York: Vintage Books, 1956), p. 6.
21. Goudsblom, *Nihilism and Culture,* p. ix.
22. Peter Unger, "Skepticism and Nihilism," *Nous* 14 (1980), 517–45, p. 517.
23. The distinction between alethiology (the "theory of the nature of truth") and epistemology (the "theory of the test for truth") was pointed out to me by Timothy Jackson. For further discussion of this point, see his "The Theory and Practice of Discomfort: Richard Rorty and Pragmatism," *Thomist* 51 (1987), pp. 270–98, esp. pp. 279ff.
24. Note that metaphysical nihilism does not deny the reality of mind or consciousness. This restriction is necessary if metaphysical nihilism is to be a real possibility—if there is no mind that makes the claim, "Nothing is real," then there is no claim made, and hence, no nihilism in this vein. This form of nihilism is usually identified as a psychological disorder. See the *Oxford English Dictionary* (second edition) entry on "nihilism," definition 2c.
25. Note that a feeling of pointlessness does not inevitably follow from the judgment that life lacks ultimate purpose or meaning; existential nihilism, as used here, requires the presence of both the judgment and the feeling.
26. Donald Crosby breaks down nihilism slightly differently; his typology includes political nihilism (by which he means, essentially, terrorism) and does not distinguish between epistemological and alethiological nihilism. This latter distinction is, however, crucial, as we shall see below.

27. Neither Barth nor Rorty identifies himself as a nihilist in any sense of the word, thereby following the long-standing "hands-off" policy in the face of nihilism. Nevertheless, the labels (as defined here) are accurate, as will be argued in Chapters Five and Six.
28. Take "There is no truth" to be the expression of alethiological nihilism. If the statement is true, then it is false, because there is at least one true statement (itself). (It is in part to avoid this problem that Rorty refrains from calling his views on truth a "position.") Epistemological nihilism—"no knowledge is possible"—only contradicts itself if it poses as knowledge.
29. See, for example, Pauline Kael's review of the film *Drugstore Cowboy* in the *New Yorker*, October 30, 1990.
30. Until recently, only the Russian nihilists and, perhaps, Max Stirner have failed to make this inference. The Russian nihilists are also, historically, the only group that sought to describe themselves as such. What is interesting about this self-designation is that, according to the typology given above, they would be eligible only for ethical nihilism. One of its contemporaries characterized Russian nihilism as the declaration of war against "everything that was not based upon pure and positive reason" (Stepniak, *Underground Russia:Revolutionary Profiles and Sketches from Life*, trans. from the Italian; London: Smith, Elder, 1883, p. 7). Nikolai Beryayev challenges even the ethical nihilism of their position, stating that "[Russian] nihilism was a movement of young people with faith. When the nihilists protested against morality, they did so in the name of goodness" (*Russian Thought in the Nineteenth and Twentieth Century*, quoted in Goudsblom, *Nihilism and Culture*, p. 8.)
31. Erasmus–Luther, *Discourse on Free Will*, trans. Ernst F. Winter (New York: Ungar, 1961). See also Richard H. Popkin, *The History of Skepticism* (Berkeley and Los Angeles: University of California Press, 1979), p. 6.
32. In practice, of course, there is little difference between an agnostic and an atheist, or between a real skeptic and a nihilist, but this merely reiterates the difference between skepticism and nihilism. Skepticism is a philosophical position, nihilism an existential or practical one. Nihilism can be seen as skepticism lived out.

33. One might say that this is also true of metaphysical nihilism, that the notion of God presumes some entity existing independently of the mind. Metaphysical nihilism is, however, consistent with an extreme form of idealistic pantheism. I could believe that nothing exists outside of my own mind while also believing that God and the world are indistinct. What this means, of course, is that I would regard myself as God.

CHAPTER 3: NIETZSCHE AND THE CRISIS OF NIHILISM

1. The almost universal agreement that Nietzsche regarded nihilism as a defining characteristic of modern culture, and his own work as an attempt in some sense to overcome it, undermines the sharp distinction Bernd Magnus has recently drawn between the "lumpers" and the "splitters" among Nietzsche scholars. Even "splitters"—scholars who restrict themselves to the published works—see nihilism as one of Nietzsche's important concerns, something they could not do solely on the basis of the remarks on nihilism in works he himself published. See Magnus, "Nietzsche's Philosophy in 1888: *The Will to Power* and the *Uebermensch*," *Journal of the History of Philosophy* 24 (1986), pp. 77–98.

2. Nietzsche was in no small measure responsible for some of the conceptual confusion that attends most twentieth-century discussions of nihilism.

3. Robert C. Solomon, in his essay, "Nietzsche, Nihilism, and Morality," in *Nietzsche: A Collection of Critical Essays*, ed. Robert C. Solomon (Notre Dame, Ind.: University of Notre Dame Press, 1980, pp. 202–25) outlines some of the ways Nietzsche used the term "nihilism," although he does not list all those given above.

4. "'I have forgotten my umbrella'," in Jacques Derrida, *Spurs/Eperons: Les Styles de Nietzsche*, bilingual edition (Chicago: University of Chicago Press, 1978), pp. 122 ff. Derrida uses this fragment in part to underscore the plurality of interpretations possible for any of Nietzsche's fragments, and the inaccessibility of any final, definitive meaning.

5. As suggested in note 1 above, there is much debate among Nietzsche scholars to what extent, if at all, one should use Nietzsche's notebooks, over against his published works. Some scholars argue that we should limit ourselves to the published works, on the grounds that only those words that Nietzsche himself committed to print can responsibly be attributed to him; only those notebook entries may be used which reduplicate issues found in the published works. See, for example, Harold Alderman, *Nietzsche's Gift* (Athens: Ohio University Press, 1977). Other scholars use freely both the notebooks and the published works. See, for example, Richard Schacht, *Nietzsche* (London: Routledge and Kegan Paul, 1983). The following analysis relies primarily on the notebooks, for the simple reason that it is only there that one finds any substantive and explicit analysis of nihilism.

6. Much like Freud, Nietzsche used an analysis of sick and diseased states to illuminate the nature of health. This is only possible if sickness and health are viewed on a continuum with one another, rather than as qualitatively different states. The examination of sickness functions as a kind of magnifier of aspects of healthy states.

7. Arthur Danto's *Nietzsche as Philosopher* (New York: Macmillan, 1965) was the first English source to develop Nietzsche's perspectivism to the point where, in Danto's eyes, it is equivalent to nihilism, the denial of truth. Contemporary French scholars—Derrida, Sarah Kofman, Maurice Blanchot, for example—have also called attention to this aspect of his thought.

8. For Nietzsche's estimation of how cautious we must be in our knowledge claims about the world, see "Let Us Beware," in *The Gay Science*, trans. Walter Kaufmann (New York: Vintage Books, 1974), pp. 167–9.

9. Nietzsche's argument appears circular here—on the one hand, all of our basic concepts stem from our belief in the ego; on the other hand, our belief in the ego stems from the structures of our language and the concepts which inform it. Fortunately, this circularity does not affect his point that our language and thinking drastically constrain the ways in which we understand the world.

10. This view of the subject as a multiplicity of warring drives is more fully developed in Book II of *Daybreak*, trans. R. J. Hollingdale (Cambridge: Cambridge University Press, 1982).

11. Thus both Buddhism and Christianity are evaluations bred of weakness for Nietzsche, in that they arise in reaction to a situation deemed intolerable as it stands—in both cases, the quality of present existence—and devalue the world in which they live as a consequence. Both are also described as nihilistic religions. (Nietzsche was not familiar with later forms of Buddhism that would be less susceptible to this charge or that offer a view of knowledge remarkably similar to his perspectivism; consider, for example, the Ch'an Buddhist's glorification of the commonplace, or Madyamika epistemology.) Nietzsche nonetheless regarded Buddhism as a healthier interpretive scheme than Christianity (or at least as the product of a higher, more refined culture), because it does not attribute an extraterrestrial, divine origin to its teachings.

12. KSA 6 *Goetzen-Daemmerung*, pp. 61–2. Cf. *The Twilight of the Idols*, in *The Portable Nietzsche*, trans. and ed. Walter Kaufmann (New York: Penguin, 1977), p. 469.

13. One wonders if this isn't because Christians on Nietzsche's model have such a low self-image that they would automatically discredit anything they create. The strong master morality, however, has confidence and self-esteem, and therefore could accept its interpretations as self-created.

14. Kierkegaard and Dostoyevsky, the two nineteenth-century "prophets" most often linked to Nietzsche, were both concerned with the consequences of Christianity's changing face, especially with its increasing "liberalization." Other thinkers also saw in Christianity's perceived demise (either through outright apostasy or the softening of its teachings) a direct tie to cultural degeneration, but most lacked the subtlety or the insight to recognize just how complex the relationship between Christianity and nihilism was (and is.) Even Dostoyevsky, who captured the nihilistic pathos so well in his portrayal of Kirolov in *The Possessed* or in Ivan Karamozov's statement, "If God is dead, then everything is permitted," offered more of a characterization of the sentiment than a critique of its causes.

15. As we shall see, this analysis has been adopted (or perhaps, co-opted) in modified form by the anti-foundationalists.

16. *The Gay Science*, pp. 181–2.

17. The parallels to Barth's attack on religion are quite striking. See below, pp. 67ff.

18. in the Third Essay, Section 24 of Nietzsche's *On the Genealogy of Morals*, trans. Walter Kaufmann (New York: Vintage Books, 1989), p. 152.

19. *Human, All-too-human*, trans. Marion Faber (Lincoln: University of Nebraska Press, 1984), III, 109, p. 78.

20. That Nietzsche saw much of his own task as destructive is clear; but it is sometimes overlooked that he saw this as a propaedeutic to creation.

21. Alexander Nehamas has recently argued that Nietzsche should be read primarily as trying to create a certain picture of who he was as an author. See his *Nietzsche: Life as Literature* (Cambridge, Mass.: Harvard University Press, 1985).

22. KSA 6, *Goetzen-Daemmerung*, pp. 96–7; *Twilight of the Idols*, in *The Portable Nietzsche*, p. 501.

23. Nietzsche did not, to my knowledge, ever distinguish between the two. He also tended to conflate together all three forms of nihilism—epistemological, alethiological, and existential. This is not surprising, since he saw all three as occurring simultaneously in the particular intellectual context in which he was writing.

24. Quotations are from *Human, All-too-human*, trans. Marion Faber, and *The Gay Science*, trans. Walter Kaufmann.

25. from Nietzsche, *Thus Spoke Zarathustra*, in *The Portable Nietzsche*, pp. 174–5.

26. *Ecce Homo: Or, How One Becomes What One Is*, in *The Basic Writings of Nietzsche*,) trans. and ed. Walter Kaufmann (New York: Random House, 1968), p. 675.

27. Because of this, *Zarathustra* tends to be underexamined. This defect in Nietzsche scholarship is being corrected, how-

ever; see Lawrence Lampert, *Nietzsche's Teaching: An Interpretation of 'Thus Spoke Zarathustra'* (New Haven: Yale University Press, 1986), and Kathleen M. Higgins, *Nietzsche's Zarathustra* (Philadelphia: Temple University Press, 1987).

28. Connected to this are Nietzsche's ideas of *amor fati* (love of fate) and the eternal recurrence. The latter, in particular, is a problematic aspect of Nietzsche's thought, since it is not clear whether Nietzsche thought that this doctrine (that all that has been and all that will be repeats itself in infinity) was literally true or simply something one should embrace and live as though it were true. In either case, the underlying point is that only a person who can affirm all the moments of the past, present and future without reservation, and can will them to repeat themselves forever, can be said to affirm life in its entirety. For a discussion of this idea within Nietzsche's thought, see Bernd Magnus, *Nietzsche's Existential Imperative* (Bloomington: Indiana University Press, 1978).

29. The only form of nihilism Nietzsche could be seen as embracing is epistemological nihilism. His analysis of the nature of knowledge seems to lead to a rejection of the possibility of knowledge, or at least, a rejection of the classic connection between knowledge and truth, for he clearly believes that knowledge does not in and of itself give us an accurate picture of the world as it is. Note, however, that if we adopt his redefinition of knowledge as an appropriative, interpretive tool, then knowledge is not only possible, but necessary for our survival. For a rejection of the view that Nietzsche is a nihilist in any sense of the term, see Richard Schacht, "Nietzsche and Nihilism," in *Nietzsche: A Collection of Critical Essays*, Ed. Robert C. Solomon (Notre Dame, Ind.: University of Notre Dame Press, 1980), pp. 58–82.

CHAPTER 4: KARL BARTH AND THE THEOLOGY OF CRISIS

1. Author's preface to the English translation of Adolf von Harnack, *What is Christianity?* trans. Thomas Bailey Saunders (Philadelphia: Fortress Press, 1986), p. vi.

2. See George Rupp, *Culture-Protestantism: German Liberal Theology at the Turn of the Twentieth Century*, (Missoula, Mont.: Scholar's Press, 1977) for an informative account of the differences between liberal theologians at that time. While Rupp convincingly argues that theological liberalism was far more varied than it appears when viewed in the shadow of neo-orthodoxy's attack on it, he does concede that there is sufficient similarity to warrant a generic name.

3. Harnack's lectures were immensely popular; by 1927 they had gone through fourteen printings and been translated into as many languages. They were also, in non-liberal circles, quite controversial, for they had significantly reduced the scope of Christianity's essence.

4. This is of course not to say that Nietzsche was without influence at this time. Georg Brandes had begun lecturing on Nietzsche in Denmark in 1888, and, after the onset of his insanity, his sister, Elizabeth Foerster-Nietzsche, devoted herself to popularizing his philosophy (albeit in radically distorted form). One finds reference to the existence of a "Nietzsche cult" as early as 1895. (See Hubert Cabcik, "Der Nietzsche-Kultus in Weimar," *Nietzsche-Studien* 16 (1987), pp. 405–29.) But theological attention to his work came later.

5. There were exceptions to this confidence. Nietzsche's friend, Franz Overbeck, condemned the culture protestantism of his contemporaries, and went so far as to say, in a phrase picked up by Barth, that theology was the "satan" of religion. See Overbeck, *Christentum und Kultur: Gedanken und Anmerkungen zur moderne Theologie*, ed. Carl A. Bernouilli (Basel: Benno Schurabe, 1919), as well as Barth's "Unsettled Questions for Theology Today," trans. Louise Pettibone Smith, in *Theology and Church* (New York: Harper and Row, 1962, pp. 55–73). The increasing pessimism of one of Harnack's contemporaries, Ernst Troeltsch, about the future of theology prompted him in 1914 to relinquish a chair in theology for one in philosophy, a fact which historians find, in hindsight, highly significant.

6. Barth did respond shortly after this to a series of fifteen questions posed by Harnack about the new theological viewpoint arising in Germany, published in *Die christliche*

Welt in 1923. See Harnack "Fuenfzehn Fragen an die Veraechter der wissenschaftlichen Theologie unter den Theologen," with an answer by Barth in volume 37, columns 6–8, 89–91, 142–44, 244–52, 305. An English translation can be found in *The Beginnings of Dialectical Theology*, vol. 1, ed. James Robinson. (Richmond, Va.: John Knox Press, 1968), pp. 165–187.

7. Barth also severely restricted his reliance on most of the critical-historical research on the New Testament, thereby changing the method of theological exegesis. While Barth thought that historical criticism was "both necessary and justified," he regarded it as "merely the first step towards a commentary" (*Romans*, p. 6). Barth's hermeneutical stance caused as much controversy as the position he discovered with it.

8. Karl Barth, "The Problem of Ethics Today," in *The Word of God and the Word of Man*, trans. Douglas Horton (New York: Harper Torchbooks, 1957), p. 146.

9. Unsympathetic critics of dialectical theology had already made this charge. See the discussion by Karl Budde in "Die 'Theologie der Krisis' und der Weltkrieg," *Die christliche Welt* 41 (1927), columns 1104–5.

10. Alister McGrath, *The Making of Modern German Christology: From the Enlightenment to Pannenberg* (New York: Basil Blackwell, 1986), p. 98.

11. James D. Smart, *The Divided Mind of Modern Theology: Karl Barth and Rudolf Bultmann, 1908–1933* (Philadelphia: Westminster Press, 1967), p. 45.

12. Karl Barth, "The Righteousness of God," in *The Word of God and the Word of Man*, p. 10.

13. The full text of this appeal can be found in Georg Friedrich Nicolai's *Biologie des Krieges. Betrachtungen eines deutschen Naturforschers* (Zurich: Art Institut O. Fuessli, 1917), pp. 7–10 (as *The Biology of War* translated by Constance A. Grande and Julian Grande, New York: The Century Company, 1918).

14. Karl Barth, "Evangelical Theology in the Nineteenth Century," trans. Thomas Wieser in *The Humanity of God* (Rich-

mond, Va.: John Knox Press, 1960), p. 14.

15. See Wolfgang Huber, "Evangelische Theologie und Kirche beim Ausbruch des Ersten Weltkriegs," in *Historische Beitraege zur Friedenforschung,* ed. Wolfgang Huber (Munich: Koesel Verlag, 1970, pp. 134–215) for a discussion of some of the particulars of this transformation. The same problem—the absolutization of the present—occurs in anti-foundationalism. See below, pp. 132ff.

16. This same sentiment prompted Barth to pen the Barmen declaration of 1934 that became the manifesto of the Confessing Church under Hitler. While the church's resistance to Hitler was unquestionably praiseworthy, we should not let our admiration color the fact that the underlying motive for their actions was less a desire to protest Hitler's treatment of the Jews than to protect the interests of the church. Had Hitler not demanded absolute allegiance—something Barth believed should only be given to God—it is unclear how the church would have reacted. For a discussion of the Barmen declaration and the relationship between the church and National Socialism, see Arthur C. Cochrane, *The Church's Confession Under Hitler* (Philadelphia: Westminster Press, 1962.)

17. Karl Barth, *Gesamtausgabe,* ed. Ursula and Jochen Fabler (Zurich: Theologischer Verlag, 1971), vol. V A: 1, p. 299. Note that as early as 1909 Barth found it difficult to preach based on the liberal theology he had been taught. See Karl Barth, "Moderne Theologie und Reichsgottesarbeit," *Zeitschrift fuer Theologie und Kirche* 19 (1909), 317–21. Barth's initial trouble arose from the implicit subjectivism of the liberal framework, which seemed to him to make impossible the general statements necessary for preaching. His hesitancy actually led him to postpone accepting a pastorate for two years, during which time he worked for Martin Rade, then editor of *Die christliche Welt.*

18. Eduard Thurneysen was at Leutwil; Friedrich Gogarten, at Stelzendorf (Thuringia).

19. The difference between the first and second editions is profound. Barth described the second edition as "completely rewritten." See Hans Frei, *The Doctrine of Revelation in the Thought of Karl Barth, 1909 to 1922,* Ph. D. diss., Yale Uni-

versity, 1956, and Henri Bouillard, *Karl Barth* for a discussion of the changes.

20. Eduard Thurneysen, *Dostoyevsky: A Theological Study*, trans. Keith R. Crim (London: The Epworth Press, 1964).

21. Friedrich Gogarten, "Between the Times," in *The Beginnings of Dialectical Theology*, vol. 1, pp. 277–82.

22. "The Crisis of Our Culture," in *The Beginnings of Dialectical Theology*, vol. 1, pp. 283–300.

23. *Gesamtausgabe*, vol. V A: 1, p. 435; English translation in *Revolutionary Theology in the Making: Barth-Thurneysen Correspondence 1914–1925*, trans. and ed. James D. Smart (Richmond, Va.: John Knox Press, 1961), p. 53.

24. In 1927 Barth portrayed himself as an innocent dunderhead who from now on will be more cautious in his actions: "When I look back on my path, it seems to me to be that of someone who, groping his way upward in a dark church tower, unexpectedly grabbed not the railing but a rope; the rope was a bell-rope and now, to his horror, he must hear how the great bell tolls over him, and not just over him. He had not intended that and he cannot and will not want it to recur" (*Die christliche Dogmatik im Entwurf*, in *Gesamtausgabe*, vol. II E: 1, pp. 7–8).

25. *Church Dogmatics*, vol. II, part 1: *The Doctrine of God*, trans. T. H. L. Parker et al., ed. G.W. Bromiley and T. F. Torrance (New York: Scribner, 1957), pp. 635ff.

26. from *Vossiche Zeitung* 13 October 1922; quoted in *Zwischen den Zeiten* 1 (1923), inside back cover.

27. Founding a journal with two other like-minded thinkers seems an odd way to prevent one's thought from becoming tied to a theological school.

28. Ironically, given dialectical theology's "*kulturfeindlich*" stance, the chief problem was Gogarten's increasing involvement with the German Christians, a movement which linked Christian revelation to National Socialism. See Walter Fuerst, ed., *Dialektische Theologie in Scheidung und Bewaehrung 1933–1936* (Munich: Chr. Kaiser Verlag, 1966) for documents relevant to the dissolution of dialectical theology.

29. Surprisingly little attention is paid to Barth's early works by the deconstructive theologians, despite the obvious similarities in strategy. In part this may be due to the subsequent direction of Barth's thought. Despite the profound impact of *Der Roemerbrief*, Barth today is primarily thought of as the author of the *Kirchliche Dogmatik*. While Barth would probably prefer this, by not considering the insights—and pitfalls—of dialectical theology, the deconstructive theologians weaken their position.

30. Paul Schempp, "Marginal Glosses on Barthianism," in *The Beginnings of Dialectical Theology*, vol. 1, p. 193.

31. Hans Frei criticizes this kind of interpretation of Barth as a "misunderstanding" in his essay, "Niebuhr's Theological Background," in *Faith and Ethics: The Theology of H. Richard Niebuhr*, ed. Paul Ramsey (New York: Harper and Brothers, 1957, pp. 9–64). Frei argues that Barth "does not intend to deny faith as an immanent state in which God is present...for to do this would mean that Barth would still share common ground with Schleiermacher's own presuppositions" (43). Yet in *Der Roemerbrief* Barth unquestionably emphasizes the negative experience of grace, and even Frei concedes that "Barth was tempted to say just this [i.e. that the "'experience' of revelation...[is] a totally negative magnitude"] in his use of the 'dialectical' method which stressed the radically indirect, negative relation between grace and the sinner's faith." While Frei is correct that Barth "never developed this point of view systematically," the others who developed the theology of crisis did. See below, pp. 77ff.

32. For Barth's distinction between these three theological approaches, see his essay, "The Word of God and the Task of the Ministry," in *The Word of God and the Word of Man*, pp. 200–8. See also Gustav Krueger, "The 'Theology of Crisis': Remarks on a Recent Movement in German Theology," *Harvard Theological Review* 19 (1926), pp. 227–58, especially pp. 239–41.

33. Barth's later comments on Kierkegaard are usually limited to wry expressions of his "unfortunate" early dependence on him. Kierkegaard is conspicuous through his absence in Barth's *Protestant Theology in the Nineteenth Century* (London: SCM Press, 1972).

34. The earliest German edition of Kierkegaard's collected works dates from 1909. Isolated titles were available in translation earlier, yet he did not find an audience until Protestant liberalism began to break down.

35. See, for example, Kierkegaard's discussion of the existing individual in *Concluding Unscientific Postscript,* trans. David F. Swenson and Walter Lowrie (Princeton: Princeton University Press, 1974), pp. 115–322, especially pp. 169–224.

36. Barth was exposed to philosophical idealism both through a careful reading of Plato and Kant, at the advice of his philosophically inclined brother, Hans Barth (*Romans,* p. 4), and at the University of Marburg, the chief seat of neo-Kantianism in Germany at that time. For a helpful discussion of the influence of Kierkegaard, Plato, and Kant on Barth's early thought, see Henri Bouillard's *Karl Barth,* pp. 104–13.

37. Schleiermacher developed this new understanding of theology in *The Christian Faith,* 2 vols., ed. H. R. Mackintosh and J. S. Stewart (New York: Harper and Row, 1965).

38. See, for example, Ernst Troeltsch, *The Absoluteness of Christianity and the History of Religions,* trans. David Reid (Richmond, Va.: John Knox Press, 1981).

39. Thus Barth was still following his liberal heritage, in a twofold sense. First, he was trying to "explain" faith, given the particular historical situation in which he found himself. Second, his method was to describe the experience of the person "on this side" of the resurrection. What differentiated Barth from his teachers was his insistence that this state can only be discussed in terms of paradox, tension. Humanly viewed, faith is always despair.

40. Barth wrote to Thurneysen in 1919, "This week I read Otto's *Idea of the Holy* with considerable delight.... It opens the way for a basic surmounting of Ritschlianism." It was marred, according to Barth, by its psychological, "theological spectator" attitude. (*Revolutionary Theology in the Making,* p. 47; cf. *Gesamtausgabe* VA: 1, p. 330.)

41. The issue of natural theology was one that separated Barth from other members of the theology of crisis and ultimately led to its dissolution. See below, pp. 80–1.

42. "The Word of God and the Task of the Ministry," in *The Word of God and the Word of Man*, p. 205.

43. See, for example, Charles I. Glicksberg, *The Literature of Nihilism* (Lewisburg, Pa.: Bucknell University Press, 1975), pp. 10ff, and Karl Jaspers' *Der Psychologie der Weltanschauungen* (Berlin: J. Springer, 1922), pp. 285–6.

44. To put this another way, pure or total nihilism cannot be humanly sustained. As we will see below, attempts to maintain it deteriorate into dogmatism.

45. This position is more clearly formulated by Bultmann in his interpretation of Barth's position. See below, pp. 77–8.

46. Hans Zahrnt, *The Question of God: Protestant Theology in the Twentieth Century*, trans. R. A. Wilson (New York: Harcourt, Brace, and World, 1967), p. 25. See also Hugh Ross Mackintosh, *Types of Modern Theology: Schleiermacher to Barth* (London: Nisbet, 1947), p. 278, as well as Frei's discussion, "Skepticism as Ally and Foe," in *The Doctrine of Revelation in the Thought of Karl Barth, 1909 to 1922* pp. 167–88.

47. Rudolf Bultmann, "Liberal Theology and the Latest Theological Movement," in *Faith and Understanding*, trans. Louise Pettibone Smith (New York: Harper and Row, 1969), pp. 28–52).

48. trans. Johann M. Stochholm in *The Theology of Rudolf Bultmann*, ed. Charles W. Kegley (New York: Harper and Row, 1966), pp. 83–103.

49. Brian Gerrish, *Tradition and the Modern World: Reformed Theology in the Nineteenth Century* (Chicago: University of Chicago Press, 1978), p. 29.

50. Hans Zahrnt, *The Question of God*, pp. 47–8.

51. Gustaf Wingren, *Theology in Conflict*, trans. Eric H. Wahlstrom (Philadelphia: Muhlenberg Press, 1958), p. 116, note 4.

52. Karl Barth, "The Problem of Ethics Today," in *The Word of God and the Word of Man*, p. 143.

53. Or at least it pushed it back one level. One can still raise the question whether existential thought more generally wasn't a function of the particular historical context in which it arose.

54. See Rudolf Bultmann, *Theology of the New Testament,* trans. Kendrick Grobel (New York: Scribner, 1951), for an existential exegesis of the Gospel; see Bultmann, "The Historicity of Man and Faith," in *Existence and Faith,* trans. Schubert Ogden (New York: Meridian, 1960, pp. 92–110), for his discussion of the relationship between Heideggerian existentialism and Christian faith.

55. Dietrich Bonhoeffer, *Letters and Papers from Prison,* ed. Eberhard Bethge (New York: Macmillan, 1967), p. 181.

56. "The Problem of Ethics Today," in *The Word of God and the Word of Man,* p. 151.

57. *Karl Barth–Rudolf Bultmann Letters, 1922–1966,* trans. Geoffrey W. Bromiley (Grand Rapids, Mich.: Eerdmans, 1981), 49–50. For the Brunner-Barth exchange on the same issue, see *Natural Theology: Comprising 'Nature and Grace' by Emil Brunner and the Reply "No!" by Karl Barth,* trans. Peter Fraenkel (London: The Centenary Press, 1947).

58. For the text of Barth and Thurneysen's resignation, see *Anfaenge der dialektischen Theologie,* vol. II. ed. Juergen Moltmann (Munich: Chr. Kaiser Verlag, 1962), pp. 313–28.

59. See, for example, *Romans,* p. 97: "Both before and after Jesus men have been discovered by [God]." Christ is still unique, however, in that he provides "the standard by which all discovery of God and all being discovered by him is made known as such."

60. William Nicholls, *Systematic and Philosophical Theology.* The Pelican Guide to Modern Theology, vol. I (Baltimore: Penguin Books, 1969), p. 141.

61. Helmut Kuhn, *Encounter with Nothingness: An Essay on Existentialism.* (Hinsdale, Ill:: Henry Regnery, 1949), p. 154.

62. Karl Barth, "The Need and Promise of Christian Preaching," in *The Word of God and the Word of Man,* pp. 97–8.

CHAPTER 5: RICHARD RORTY AND THE DISSOLUTION OF CRISIS

1. This ethos resurfaced theologically during this time as well in Death-of-God theology. See, for example, Thomas J. Altizer's *The Gospel of Christian Atheism* (Philadelphia: Westminster Press, 1966). More extreme and one-dimensional than the theology of crisis, the movement was short-lived.

2. Jean-Paul Sartre, "L'existentialisme est un humanisme," trans. as "Existentialism" in *Existentialism and Human Emotions* (New York: Philosophical Library, 1957). While not, philosophically speaking, one of Sartre's more sophisticated works, it captures the popular understanding of existentialism. It was also the occasion for Heidegger's rejection of any association with existentialism. See Martin Heidegger, "Letter on Humanism," in *Basic Writings*, ed. D. F. Krell (New York: Harper and Row, 1977). Compare Sartre's position to that of Kierkegaard, who argued that the full extent of human responsibility was not revealed until the individual stood alone before God. Sartre fell prey to the simple-minded "either-religion-or-freedom" dichotomy.

3. Some of the other names include "textualism," "postmodernism," "neo-pragmatism," "anti-foundationalism," and the "new historicism."

4. Roger Lundin, "Deconstructive Therapy," *The Reformed Journal* 36:1 (1986), p. 15.

5. Richard Bernstein, *Beyond Objectivism and Relativism: Science, Hermeneutics, and Praxis* (Philadelphia: University of Pennsylvania Press, 1985), p. 18. Bernstein traces this distress back to Descartes' search for a foundation, an indubitable ground for knowledge; hence the adjective, "Cartesian."

6. These exceptions are the Russian nihilists, whose avid materialism distinguishes their usage of "nihilism" from almost every other, and Max Stirner, the left-wing Hegelian, whose *Das Ich und Sein Eigenes* (English translation, *The Ego and His Own*, London: A.C. Fifield, 1913) is probably the most frankly nihilistic work ever written.

7. The phrase is drawn from Christopher Norris' *The Deconstructive Turn: Essays in the Rhetoric of Philosophy* (New York: Methuen, 1984).

8. Jean-François Lyotard. *The Postmodern Condition: A Report on Knowledge*, trans. Geoff Bennington and Brian Massumi (Minneapolis: University of Minnesota Press, 1984), p. 41.

9. The range of names used to identify this sensibility points to its many faces. Although "deconstruction" is often used generically to include both Derrida and Rorty, for clarity's sake its range is restricted here to Derrida and those directly influenced by him; "anti- foundationalism" is used to refer to Rorty and his circle.

10. Richard Rorty, *Philosophy and the Mirror of Nature*, (Princeton: Princeton University Press, 1979), p. 3.

11. See Thomas S. Kuhn, *The Structure of Scientific Revolutions*, 2nd ed. (Chicago: University of Chicago Press, 1970), as well as Rorty, *Philosophy and the Mirror of Nature*, pp. 322–42.

12. What counts as justification in Rorty's scheme of things is laid out below. See pp. 103–4, 108–9.

13. An analogous case would be linking Christian ethics to belief in the trinity: It is surely possible to have one without the other. In fact, one could argue that the dogmatic insistence on belief in the trinity prompts an intolerance inimical to the true nature of Christianity. This kind of argument was widely made by the Protestant liberals.

14. In part the controversy was due to the perceived "defection" of an analytic philosopher to the Continental tradition. But this could not account for the stir created beyond analytic circles.

15. His earlier remarks, however, make either possibility equally *im*possible, for systematic philosophy always prompts a reaction, the reaction being parasitic in turn upon the systematic movement.

16. Richard Rorty, *Consequences of Pragmatism* (Minneapolis: University of Minnesota Press, 1982).

17. *"Introduction: Pragmatism and Philosophy,"* Consequences of Pragmatism, p. xix.

18. These two ways of reading Rorty, depending upon which element of his thought one stresses, were pointed out by Van A. Harvey in an unpublished paper given at the American Academy of Religion, San Francisco, December 1981.

19. Note that Rorty's reading of the history of philosophy is far from uncontested. See, for example, Alasdair MacIntyre, "Philosophy, the 'Other' Disciplines, and Their Histories: A Rejoinder to Richard Rorty," *Soundings* 65 (1982), pp. 127–45.

20. One way of distinguishing the various strands among postmodern thought is precisely in terms of the seriousness with which different thinkers view the dissolution of foundations. Most theological exponents of postmodernism view the dissolution of absolutes as a matter of crisis and alarm. Mark C. Taylor, for example, shares Derrida's reading of the "logocentrism" of the western tradition, but unlike Rorty he regards the result of this as "unsettling," hoping only that "obscure writings" like Derrida's "might, at least for a while, help to delay and defer the terrifying arrival of the end" (in "Descartes, Nietzsche, and the Search for the Unsayable," *New York Times Book Review*, February 1, 1987, p. 4.) That the theological variants of postmodernism differ from Rorty in this regard is not surprising; Chapter Six below will argue that only if one takes nihilism seriously is religious or ethical transformation possible.

21. Deconstruction's popularity in literary circles in particular is in large part due to its attempt to view philosophy as a kind of fiction writing, which has interesting implications both for philosophical and literary writing. The relationship between literature and philosophy is the subject of a great deal of current attention. See, for example, *Literature and the Question of Philosophy*, ed. Anthony J. Cascardi (Baltimore: Johns Hopkins University Press, 1987), *Literature as Philosophy, Philosophy as Literature*, ed. Donald G. Marshall (Iowa City: University of Iowa Press, 1987), as well as the journal *Philosophy and Literature*, founded in 1976. Note, however, that existentialism broke down many of the barriers between philosophy and literature long before deconstruction entered the scene.

22. Rorty left the philosophy department at Princeton University to take a chair in the Humanities at the University of Virginia.

23. Jacques Derrida, "Tympan," in *Margins of Philosophy*, trans. Alan Bass (Chicago: University of Chicago Press, 1982), pp. ix–xxix.

24. Jacques Derrida, *Positions*, trans. Alan Bass (Chicago: University of Chicago Press, 1981), p. 17.

25. Derrida, *Positions*, p. 6.

26. See Saussure, *Course in General Linquistics*, ed. Charles Balyy and Albert Sechehaye, trans. Roy Harris (London: Duckworth, 1983).

27. An important element of Derrida's coinage of the word *différance* is that it can only be distinguished from the "correct" *différence* visually, for the pronunciation of the two words is the same. This indirectly underscores his well-known point that "writing is prior to speech." His claim is not the historically absurd one that people learned to write before they learned to talk, but that written texts rather than the spoken word are a more accurate paradigm for understanding the interpretive process, for the inherent ambiguity of this process is more fully apparent.

28. Derrida, *Positions*, p. 26

29. Richard Bernstein offers an interpretation of Derrida as an ethically motivated thinker because part of Derrida's concern is to invert traditional power hierarchies. See "Serious Play: The Ethical-Political Horizon of Jacques Derrida," *Journal of Speculative Philosophy* 1 (1987) pp. 93–117.

30. "Deconstruction and the Other," in *Dialogues with Contemporary Continental Thinkers: The Pheonomenological Heritage* ed. Richard Kearney (Manchester: Manchester University Press, 1984), p. 116.

31. Jacques Derrida, "Différance," in *Margins of Philosophy*, p. 27; for Derrida's remarks on negative theology, see p. 6. For a discussion of the connections between Derrida's thought and negative theology, see Susan Handelman, "Jacques Derrida and the Heretic Hermeneutic," in *Displacement: Derrida and After*, ed. Mark Krupnick (Bloomington: Indiana University Press, 1983), pp. 98–129.

32. The phrase is Rorty's and describes his view of "North Atlantic democracies." See "Postmodernist Bourgeois Liber-

alism" in *Hermeneutics and Praxis*, ed. Robert Hollinger (Notre Dame, Ind.: University of Notre Dame Press, 1985), pp. 214–21.

33. "Nineteenth-Century Idealism and Twentieth-Century Textualism," in *Consequences of Pragmatism*, p. 140.

34. "Nineteenth-Century Idealism and Twentieth-Century Textualism," pp. 150–1. Note that for Rorty, no theological use of deconstruction would be possible.

35. Rorty, "Deconstruction and Circumvention," *Critical Inquiry* 11 (1984), p. 3.

36. That Derrida does not express his views in this fashion makes one wonder how accurate Rorty's interpretation is: Is Derrida trying to both have his cake and eat it too, by presuming that which he himself denies? Or is he trying to avoid doing exactly this? Note that Rorty himself is liable to be asked the first question; see below, pp. 109–10.

37. The appeal to temperament parallels James' distinction between "tough-minded" and "tender-minded" philosophers. See "The Present Dilemma in Philosophy," in *The Writings of William James*, ed. John J. McDermott (Chicago: University of Chicago Press, 1977), pp. 362–76.

38. Although Rorty speaks about the pragmatist as though Rorty were a disinterested observer, we may safely regard the pragmatist as his mouthpiece. By discussing not his own view but that of some unknown "pragmatist," he avoids presenting anything that can easily be identified as his philosophical position.

39. Rorty, "Solidarity or Objectivity?" in *Post-Analytic Philosophy*, ed. John Rajchman and Cornel West (New York: Columbia University Press, 1985), pp. 3–19. More recently, Rorty has recast this distinction in terms of "ironists" and "metaphysicians"; see *Contingency, Irony, and Solidarity* (Cambridge: Cambridge University Press, 1989), especially pp. 73–95.

40. Rorty, "Hermeneutics, General Studies, and Teaching," in *Selected Papers from the Synergos Seminars* 2 (1982), 1–15.

41. Rorty's reading of Nietzsche is not uncommon, but shares with many others the defect of ignoring Nietzsche's own oft-

stated commitment to the truth imperative. Admittedly, Nietzsche's relationship to truth is ambiguous, as I have discussed in Chapter Two, but it is important not to overlook the positive things he said about truth.

42. Rorty, "Pragmatism, Relativism, and Irrationalism," p. 66.

43. Rorty, "Introduction," *Consequences of Pragmatism*, pp. xlii–xliii.

44. See, for example, Stanley Rosen's "Review of *Philosophy and the Mirror of Nature*," *Review of Metaphysics* 33 (1980), p. 802; Edward Santurri's review of Jeffrey Stout's *The Flight from Authority*, *Religious Studies Review* 9 (1983), 330–4; Colin Campbell, "The Tyranny of the Yale Critics," *New York Times Magazine* February 9, 1986; Kenneth Woodward, "A New Look at Lit Crit," *Newsweek* June 22, 1981, pp. 80–3; Harold Fromm, "Sparrows and Scholars: Literary Criticism and the Sanctification of Data," *the Georgia Review* 33:1 (1979), pp. 262, 269–70; Gerald Graff, "Fear and Trembling at Yale," *The American Scholar* 46 (1977), pp. 467–8.

45. Unfortunately, critics accusing deconstructionists or antifoundationalists of nihilism usually do not specify the particular breed of nihilism they are guilty of. Note, by the way, the similarities between the response to deconstructive strategies and the response to German idealism discussed above. Also note the absence of the fifth strand, existential nihilism.

46. See, for example, Campbell's "The Tyranny of the Yale Critics," in which Miller gets "angry" at the charge of nihilism, but says nothing more. See also Jeffrey Stout's "A Lexicon of Postmodernism" in *Religious Studies Review* 13 (1987), 18–22. Stout acknowledges that his view is often described as nihilistic but merely dismisses this as "false." A more recent work by Stout attempts to deflect the triple charges of nihilism, relativism, and skepticism that attend his work. His rebuttal of the nihilist charge is not addressed here because in that work he wishes to distinguish himself from Rorty—and indeed implies that Rorty is perhaps guilty of at least some of these accusations. See *Ethics After Babel: The Languages of Morals and Their Discontents* (Boston: Beacon Press, 1988), especially pp. 243–65.

47. Bela Egyed suggests that the absence of any rebuttal by Derrida to the charge of nihilism stems from his "insistence that we can never take our distance from nihilism because all such distancing is already caught up in nihilism" (in "Tracing Nihilism: Heidegger to Nietzsche to Derrida," in *Nietzsche and the Rhetoric of Nihilism*, Bela Egyed, ed. (Ottawa: Carleton University Press, 1989), p. 10). If Egyed is correct, this seems to me more of a conceding of the charge of nihilism than a response to it.

48. *Deconstruction and Criticism* (New York: Seabury Press, 1979), pp. 216–53.

49. See, for example, "Nineteenth-Century Idealism and Twentieth-Century Textualism," pp. 156ff; "Introduction," *Consequences of Pragmatism*, p. xlii.

50. However, there are problems with this charitable interpretation, as well. Unless Rorty believes that the claim that there are no deep structures to the world was true, it would not serve to liberate us from a way of viewing the world that was false. There are no deep structures to the universe, no way it "really" is, we are told. And this should provoke no crisis, for only if we (falsely) believe there are deep structures do we experience their perceived absence as a problem. To be disturbed by these claims, we have to be committed to an idea of "getting things right" that is no longer intellgible.

    The difficulty, though, is that unless we care about getting things right, we will not experience as liberating any recognition of the falsity of these earlier misbegotten views. We find ourselves in the contradictory position of having to care about the deep structure of things in order to be relieved that no such structures exist. The upshot seems to be that if Rorty persuades us not to care, we have no reason to take his claims seriously.

51. For a very helpful discussion of Rorty's stance against theory, see C. G. Prado, *The Limits of Pragmatism* (Atlantic Highlands, N.J.: Humanities International Press, 1987).

52. Rorty, *Philosophy and the Mirror of Nature*, p. 176.

53. Consider, for example, how each of these communities might assess the notion of the "canon," currently under such scrutiny.

54. See, for example, Peter L. Berger and Thomas Luckmann, *The Social Construction of Reality: A Treatise in the Sociology of Knowledge* (New York: Irvington, 1980).

55. Rorty, "Postmodernist Bourgeois Liberalism," p. 214.

56. A similar criticism has been made by Richard Bernstein in "One Step Forward, Two Steps Backward," *Political Theory* 15 (1987), p. 548. "Given Rorty's constant appeal to history and historicism, he ignores the *historical fact* that we are confronted with conflicting and incompatible practices—even in so-called liberal democracy."

57. Rorty, "Nineteenth-Century Idealism and Twentieth-Century Textualism," p. 158.

58. Rorty, "Hermeneutics, General Studies, and Teaching," p. 5.

59. Rorty, *Philosophy and the Mirror of Nature*, p. 340.

CHAPTER 6: DISCONTENTED VERSUS UNREPENTANT NIHILISTS

1. In the course of his authorship Kierkegaard distinguished between three basic modes of existence: the aesthetic, the ethical, and the religious; within the religious mode, he distinguished further between religiousness *a* and religiousness *b* (paganism and Christianity). Some have argued that there were also gradations within the ethical mode. See, for example, Gregor Malantschuk, *Kierkegaard's Thought*, trans. Howard V. Hong and Edna H. Hong (Princeton: Princeton University Press, 1974), pp. 83–91.

2. Although Kierkegaard believed there to be profound differences between the ethical and the religious modes (see *Fear and Trembling*, trans. Howard V. Hong and Edna H. Hong, Princeton: Princeton University Press, 1983), he frequently grouped the two together because both are marked by a commitment to something beyond the temporal realm, which the aesthetic mode lacks.

3. Rorty, *Contingency, Irony, and Solidarity*, p. 22.

4. The only real difference is that, as Kierkegaard paints the characters, their attempt to maintain the "interesting" in

life is tinged with pathos, since it is bound to come to grief. Kierkegaard had a clearly polemical intention in his portrayal of the aesthetic mode.

5. This, of course, was part of what scared Barth away from dialectical theology: the reification of dialectics into another instance of theological hubris that claimed the possession of God could be gained through the logical manipulation of concepts. Much like Derrida and Rorty, the early Barth wished to avoid the systematization of his thinking into a philosophical or theological position. See above, Chapter Four, pp. 80–4.

6. The loss of truth, conventionally understood, does not, in Rorty's eyes, entail the loss of knowledge, for knowledge is simply justified (according to the warrants of the community to which one belongs) belief. See above, Chapter Five, pp. 107–9.

7. Rorty, "On Ethnocentrism: A Reply to Clifford Geertz," *Michigan Quarterly Review* 25 (Summer 1986), pp. 525–34, especially p. 531.

8. For a fuller articulation of a similar position, see Jeffrey Stout, *Ethics After Babel* (Boston: Beacon Press, 1988). Although his position is similar to Rorty's in many respects, Stout wishes to distance himself at least from Rorty's alethiological nihilism. Stout agrees that "knowledge" is best understood simply as "justified belief" but also asserts that he believes in "truth." See especially pp. 243–65.

9. See Arthur Danto, *Nietzsche as Philosopher*; Richard Schacht, "Nietzsche and Nihilism"; Robert C. Solomon, "Nietzsche, Nihilism, and Morality"; Maurice Blanchot, "The Limits of Experience: Nihilism," in *The New Nietzsche*, ed. David B. Allison (New York: Dell, 1979), pp. 121–7; *Nietzsche and the Rhetoric of Nihilism*, ed. Bela Egyed et al.

10. On Nietzsche's affinities with postmodernism, see, for example, Bernd Magnus, "Nietzsche and Postmodern Criticism," *Nietzsche Studien* 18 (1989), pp. 301–16. On Nietzsche as a religious thinker, see Paul Valadier, "Christliche Dekadenz und Wiederaufleben des Goettlichen: Die Ambivalenz Nietzsches und der Nietzsche-Interpretation," *Stimmen der Zeit* 196:6 (June 1978), 395–406.

11. One way to describe the two strands of Nietzsche interpretation is to consider how each view sees Nietzsche responding to the claim, "If there is no truth, then all is meaningless." The aesthetic interpretation would have Nietzsche rejecting the conclusion, arguing that the absence of truth does not entail meaninglessness. The ethical-religious interpretation has Nietzsche rejecting the premise: Simply because the Platonic-Christian interpretation of the world has collapsed does not mean that there is no truth, only that one alleged truth (the truth of Christianity) has been shown to be false. There certainly are or could be others.

12. Bouillard, *Karl Barth*, p. 103.

13. Rorty, "From Logic to Language to Play: A Plenary Address to the Inter-American Congress," *Proceedings and Addresses of the American Philosophical Association* 59 (1986), p. 753. In statements like these, Rorty is clearly making (negative) assertions about the nature of the world, and thus has moved beyond skepticism into nihilism.

14. In a review of Rorty's *Philosophy and the Mirror of Nature,* Stanley Rosen quips that Rorty's "cheerful nihilism" is certainly preferable to grim or depressed nihilism ("Review of *Philosophy and the Mirror of Nature,*" *Review of Metaphysics* 33 (1980), 799–802). However, not only is such a preference a matter of no little controversy, as we have seen, but there is something oxymoronic about the phrase "cheerful nihilism," given its earlier usage. See above, pp. 14–5.

15. In *Post-Analytic Philosophy,* p. 259.

16. Thomas McCarthy, "Private Irony and Public Decency: Richard Rorty's New Pragmatism," *Critical Inquiry* 16 (1990), p. 367.

17. "One Step Forward, Two Steps Backward: Richard Rorty on Liberal Democracy and Philosophy," p. 541.

18. For other versions of this criticism, see Christopher Norris, *The Contest of Faculties* (London: Methuen, 1981), especially ch. 6; Rebecca Comay, "Interrupting the Conversation: Notes on Rorty," in *Anti-Foundationalism and Practical Reasoning,* ed. Evan Simpson (Edmonton, Alberta: Academic Printing and Publishing, 1987); Alfonso J. Damico, "The Politics After Deconstruction: Rorty, Dewey, and Marx," in

Context over Foundation: Dewey and Marx, ed. William J. Gavin (Boston: D. Reidel, 1988), pp. 177–205.

19. Rorty, "Truth and Freedom: A Reply to Thomas McCarthy," *Critical Inquiry* 16 (1990), p. 634.

20. A similar argument is made by McCarthy in the essay already cited.

21. The troubling implications of this view are all the more apparent when one realizes that more serious questions (for example, the age at which a fetus becomes a person or whether there are conditions under which torture is acceptable) are likewise simply matters of community preference. While one might think that this would mean that the politeness deemed appropriate in discussions of aesthetics would then extend to discussions about abortion, the reverse would more likely happen—people would take disputes about art and music as seriously as they now take disputes about abortion.

22. See Jeffrey Stout, "Liberal Society and the Language of Morals," *Soundings* 69 (1986), pp. 32–59, especially p. 45.

23. See, for example, Juergen Habermas, *Theory of Communicative Action*, trans. Thomas McCarthy (Boston: Beacon Press, 1984).

24. Published as "The Structure and Content of Truth," *The Journal of Philosophy* 87:6 (1990), pp. 279–328.

25. See, for example, Mark C. Taylor, *Erring: A Postmodern A/theology* (Chicago: University of Chicago Press, 1984), and Joseph Stephen O'Leary, *Questioning Back: The Overcoming of Metaphysics in the Christian Tradition* (Minneapolis: Winston Press, 1985).

Selected Bibliography

Alderman, Harold. *Nietzsche's Gift.* Athens: Ohio University Press, 1977.

Altizer, Thomas J. *The Gospel of Christian Atheism.* Philadelphia: Westminster Press, 1966.

Arapura, J. G. *Religion as Anxiety and Tranquillity.* Mouton: The Hague, 1972.

Aschheim, Steven E. "After the Death of God: Varieties of Nietzschean Religion." *Nietzsche Studien* 17 (1988), pp. 218–49.

Atkins, G. Douglas. "'Count it All Joy': The Affirmative Nature of Deconstruction." *University of Hartford Studies in Literature* 16 (1984), pp. 120–8.

———. "J. Hillis Miller, Deconstruction, and the Recovery of Transcendence." *Notre Dame English Journal: A Journal of Religion in Literature* 13:1 (1980), 51–63.

Barth, Karl. *Church Dogmatics.* 5 vols. Trans. T. H. L. Parker et al. Ed. G. W. Bromiley and T. F. Torrance. New York: Scribner, 1936–1969.

———. *Epistle to the Romans.* Trans. Edwyn Hoskyns from the 6th German edition, 1933; rpt. Oxford: Oxford University Press, 1977.

———. "Evangelical Theology in the Nineteenth Century." Trans. Thomas Wieser. In *The Humanity of God.* Richmond, Va.: John Knox Press, 1960, pp. 11–33.

———. *Gesamtausgabe.* Ed. Ursula and Jochen Fabler. Zurich: Theologischer Verlag, 1971.

———. "Moderne Theologie und Reichsgottesarbeit." *Zeitschrift fuer Theologie und Kirche* 19 (1909), 317–21.

———. "The Need and Promise of Christian Preaching." In *The Word of God and the Word of Man.* Trans. Douglas Horton. New York: Harper Torchbooks, 1957, pp. 97–135.

———. "The Problem of Ethics Today." In *The Word of God and the Word of Man.* Trans. Douglas Horton. New York: Harper Torchbooks, 1957, pp. 136–82.

———. *Protestant Theology in the Nineteenth Century: Its Background and History.* London: SCM Press, 1972.

———. "The Righteousness of God." In *The Word of God and the Word of Man.* Trans. Douglas Horton. New York: Harper Torchbooks, 1957, pp. 9–27.

———. "Unsettled Questions for Theology Today." In *Theology and Church.* Trans. Louise Pettibone Smith. New York: Harper and Row, 1962, pp. 55–73.

———. "The Word of God and the Task of the Ministry." In *The Word of God and the Word of Man.* Trans. Douglas Horton. New York: Harper Torchbooks, 1957, pp. 183–217.

Barth, Karl and Rudolf Bultmann. *Karl Barth–Rudolf Bultmann: Letters, 1922–1966.* Trans. Geoffrey W. Bromiley. Ed. Bernd Jaspert and Geoffrey W. Bromiley. Grand Rapids, Mich.: Eerdmans, 1981.

———. Barth, Karl and Eduard Thurneysen. *Revolutionary Theology in the Making: Barth-Thurneysen Correspondence 1914–1925.* Trans. James D. Smart. Richmond, Va.: John Knox Press, 1961.

Berger, Peter L. and Thomas Luckmann. *The Social Construction of Reality: A Treatise in the Sociology of Knowledge.* New York: Irvington, 1980.

Bernasconi, Robert. "Deconstruction and the Possibility of Ethics." In *Deconstruction and Philosophy: The Texts of Jacques Derrida.* Ed. John Sallis. Chicago: University of Chicago Press, 1987, pp. 122–39.

Bernstein, Richard. *Beyond Objectivism and Relativism: Science, Hermeneutics, and Praxis.* Philadelphia: University of Pennsylvania Press, 1985.

———. "One Step Forward, Two Steps Backward: Richard Rorty on Liberal Democracy and Philosophy." *Political Theory* 15 (1987), pp. 538–63.

———. *Philosophical Profiles: Essays in a Pragmatic Mode.* Philadelphia: University of Pennsylvania Press, 1986.

———. "Serious Play: The Ethical-Political Horizon of Jacques Derrida." *Journal of Speculative Philosophy* 1 (1987), pp. 93–117.

Blanchot, Maurice. "The Limits of Experience: Nihilism." In *The New Nietzsche.* Ed. David B. Allison. New York: Dell, 1979, pp. 121–7.

Blocker, Gene. *The Meaning of Meaninglessness.* The Hague: Martinus Nijhoff, 1974.

Bloom, Allan. *The Closing of the American Mind.* New York: Simon and Schuster, 1987.

Bonhoeffer, Dietrich. *Letters and Papers from Prison.* Ed. Ebelhard Bethge. New York: Macmillan, 1967.

Bouillard, Henri. *Genèse et évolution de la théologie dialectique,* vol. I of *Karl Barth.* Paris: Aubier, 1957.

Brunner, Emil and Karl Barth. *Natural Theology: Comprising 'Nature and Grace' and the Reply "No!"* Trans. Peter Fraenkel. London: The Centenary Press, 1947.

Budde, Karl. "Die 'Theologie der Krisis' und der Weltkrieg." *Die christliche Welt* 41 (1927), cols. 1104–5.

Bultmann, Rudolf. "The Historicity of Man and Faith." In *Existence and Faith: Shorter Writings of Rudolf Bultmann.* Trans. Schubert Ogden. New York: Meridian, 1960, pp. 92–110.

———. "Liberal Theology and the Latest Theological Movement." Trans. Louise Pettibone Smith. In *Faith and Understanding.* New York: Harper and Row, 1969, pp. 28–52.

———. *Theology of the New Testament.* Trans. Kendrick Grobel. New York: Scribner, 1951.

Cabcik, Hubert. "Der Nietzsche-Kultus in Weimar." *Nietzsche Studien* 16 (1987), 405–29.

Campbell, Colin. "The Tyranny of the Yale Critics." *New York Times Magazine* February 9, 1986.

Camus, Albert. *The Myth of Sisyphus and Other Essays.* Trans. Justin O'Brien. New York: Vintage Books, 1955.

———. *The Rebel: An Essay on Man in Revolt.* Trans. Anthony Bower. New York: Vintage Books, 1956.

Carr, Karen L. "Nietzsche on Nihilism and the Crisis of Interpretation." *Soundings* 73 (1990), 85–104.

Cochrane, Arthur C. *The Church's Confession Under Hitler.* Philadelphia: Westminster, 1962.

Comay, Rebecca. "Interrupting the Conversation: Notes on Rorty." In *Anti-Foundationalism and Practical Reasoning.* Ed. Evan Simpson. Edmonton, Alberta: Academic Printing and Publishing, 1987, pp. 83–98.

Crosby, Donald A. *The Specter of the Absurd: Sources and Criticisms of Modern Nihilism.* Albany: State University of New York Press, 1988.

Damico, Alfonso J. "The Politics After Deconstruction: Rorty, Dewey, and Marx." In *Context over Foundation: Dewey and Marx.* Ed. William J. Gavin. Boston: D. Reidel, 1988, pp. 177–205.

Danto, Arthur. *Nietzsche as Philosopher.* New York: Macmillan, 1965.

Davidson, Donald. "The Structure and Content of Truth." *Journal of Philosophy* 87:6 (1990), pp. 279–328.

Dean, William. "The Challenge of the New Historicism." *Journal of Religion* 66 (1986), 261–81.

Derrida, Jacques. "Deconstruction and the Other." In *Dialogues with Contemporary Continental Thinkers: The Phenomenological Heritage.* Ed. Richard Kearney.

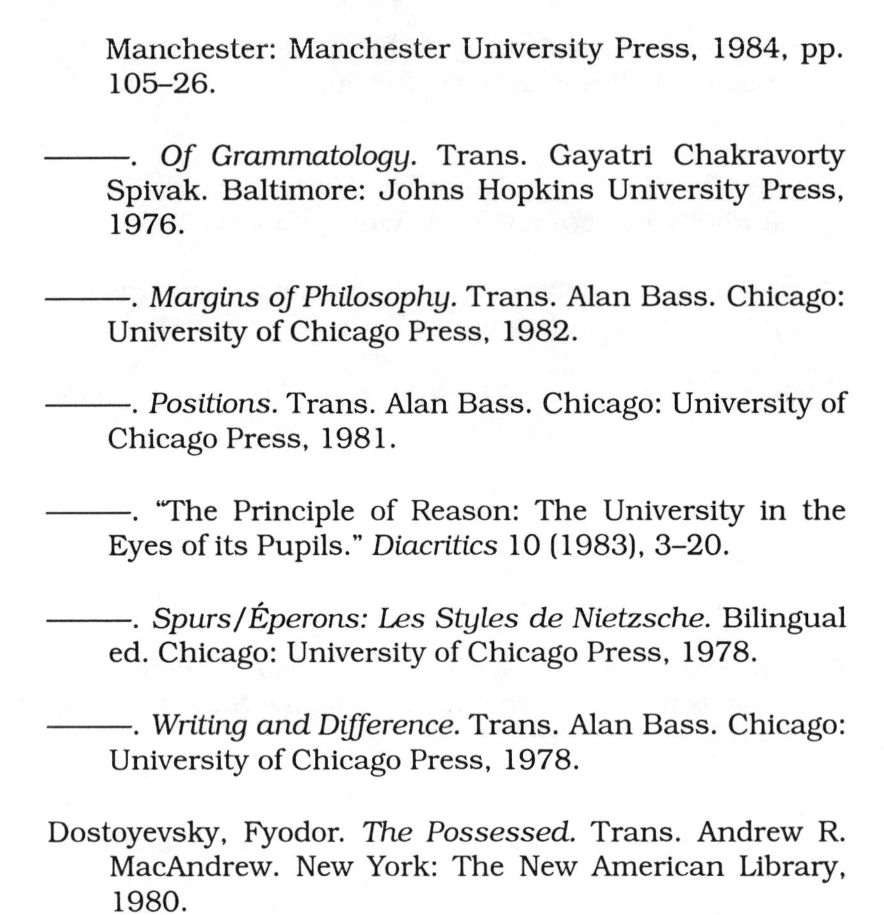

Manchester: Manchester University Press, 1984, pp. 105–26.

———. *Of Grammatology*. Trans. Gayatri Chakravorty Spivak. Baltimore: Johns Hopkins University Press, 1976.

———. *Margins of Philosophy*. Trans. Alan Bass. Chicago: University of Chicago Press, 1982.

———. *Positions*. Trans. Alan Bass. Chicago: University of Chicago Press, 1981.

———. "The Principle of Reason: The University in the Eyes of its Pupils." *Diacritics* 10 (1983), 3–20.

———. *Spurs/Éperons: Les Styles de Nietzsche*. Bilingual ed. Chicago: University of Chicago Press, 1978.

———. *Writing and Difference*. Trans. Alan Bass. Chicago: University of Chicago Press, 1978.

Dostoyevsky, Fyodor. *The Possessed*. Trans. Andrew R. MacAndrew. New York: The New American Library, 1980.

Egyed, Bela, ed. *Nietzsche and the Rhetoric of Nihilism*. Ottawa: Carleton University Press, 1989.

Frei, Hans. *The Doctrine of Revelation in the Thought of Karl Barth, 1909 to 1922: The Nature of Barth's Break with Liberalism*. Ph. D. diss., Yale University, 1956.

———. "Niebuhr's Theological Background." In *Faith and Ethics: The Theology of H. Richard Niebuhr*. Ed. Paul Ramsey. New York: Harper and Brothers, 1957, pp. 9–64.

Fromm, Harold. "Sparrows and Scholars: Literary Criticism and the Sanctification of Data." *The Georgia Review.* 33:1 (1979), 255–76.

Fuerst, Walter, ed. *Dialektische Theologie in Scheidung und Bewaehrung 1933–1936.* Munich: Chr. Kaiser Verlag, 1966.

Gerrish, Brian. *Tradition and the Modern World: Reformed Theology in the Nineteenth Century.* Chicago: University of Chicago Press, 1978.

Glicksberg, Charles I. *The Literature of Nihilism.* Lewisburg: Bucknell University Press, 1975.

Goerdt, W. "Nihilismus." In *Historisches Woerterbuch der Philosophie.* Ed. Joachim Ritter and Karlfried Gruender. Darmstadt: Wissenschaftliche Buchgesellschaft, 1984.

Gogarten, Friedrich. "Between the Times." In *The Beginnings of Dialectical Theology,* vol I. Trans. James M. Robinson. Richmond, Va.: John Knox Press, 1968, pp. 277–82.

———. "The Crisis of Our Culture." In *The Beginnings of Dialectical Theology,* vol. I. Trans. James M. Robinson. Richmond, Va.: John Knox Press, 1968, pp. 283–300.

Goudsblom, Johan. *Nihilism and Culture.* Totowa, N.J.: Rowman and Littlefield, 1980.

Graff, Gerald. "Fear and Trembling at Yale." *The American Scholar* 46 (1977), 467–78.

Habermas, Juergen. *Theory of Communicative Action.* Trans. Thomas McCarthy. Boston: Beacon Press, 1984.

Handelman, Susan. "Jacques Derrida and the Heretic Hermeneutic." In *Displacement: Derrida and After.* Ed. Mark Krupnick. Bloomington: Indiana University Press, 1983, pp. 98–129.

Harnack, Adolf von. "Fuenfzen Fragen an die Veraechter der wissenschaftlichen Theologie unter den Theologen." *Die christliche Welt* 37 (1923), cols. 6–8, 89–91, 142–4, 244–52, 305.

———. *What is Christianity?* Trans. Thomas Bailey Saunders. Philadelphia: Fortress Press, 1986.

Harvey, Van Austin. "Remarks on Rorty." Paper presented at American Academy of Religion, San Francisco, December 1981.

Hegel, G. W. f. *Faith and Knowledge.* Trans. Walter Cerf and H. S. Harris. Albany: State University of New York Press, 1977.

Heidegger, Martin. *Being and Time.* Trans. Edward Robinson and John Macquarrie. New York: Harper and Row, 1962.

———. "Letter on Humanism." In *Basic Writings from 'Being and Time' (1927) to 'The Task of Thinking' (1964).* Ed. D. F. Krell. New York: Harper and Row, 1979.

Higgins, Kathleen. *Nietzsche's Zarathustra.* Philadelphia: Temple University Press, 1987.

Huber, Wolfgang. "Evangelische Theologie und Kirche beim Ausbruch des Ersten Weltkriegs." In *Historische Beitraege zur Friedenforschung.* Ed. Wolfgang Huber. Studien zur Friedenforschung 4. Munich: Koesel Verlag, 1970, pp. 134–215.

Jackson, Timothy. "The Theory and Practice of Discomfort: Richard Rorty and Pragmatism." *Thomist* 51 (1987), 270–98.

Jacobi, Friedrich Heinrich. "Sendschriften an Fichte." In *Werke.* Ed. Friedrich Roth and Friedrich Koeppen. Darmstadt: Wissenschaftliche Buchgesellschaft, 1968, pp. 3–57.

Jaspers, Karl. *Psychologie der Weltanschauungen.* Berlin: J. Springer, 1922.

Juenger, Ernst. *Ueber die Linie.* Frankfurt: Vittorio Klostermann, 1950.

Kierkegaard, Soren. *Concluding Unscientific Postscript.* Trans. David F. Swenson and Walter Lowrie. Princeton: Princeton University Press, 1974.

———. *Either/Or.* Trans. Walter Lowrie. Princeton: Princeton University Press, 1972.

———. *Fear and Trembling.* Trans. Howard V. Hong and Edna H. Hong. Princeton: Princeton University Press, 1983.

Koester, Peter. "Nietzsche-Kritik und Nietzsche-Rezeption in der Theologie des 20. Jahrhundert." *Nietzsche Studien* 10/11 (1981/2), pp. 615–85.

Kraft, William F. *A Psychology of Nothingness.* Philadelphia: Westminster Press, 1974.

Krueger, Gustav. "The 'Theology of Crisis': Remarks on a Recent Movement in German Theology." *Harvard Theological Review* 19 (1926), pp. 227–58.

Kuhn, Helmut. *Encounter with Nothingness: An Essay on Existentialism.* Hinsdale, Ill.: Henry Regnery, 1949.

Kuhn, Thomas S. *The Structure of Scientific Revolutions*. Chicago: University of Chicago Press, 1970.

Lampert, Lawrence. *Nietzsche's Teaching: An Interpretation of 'Thus Spoke Zarathustra'*. New Haven: Yale University Press, 1986.

Levin, David Michael. *The Opening of Vision: Nihilism and the Postmodern Situation*. New York: Routledge and Kegan Paul, 1988.

Loewith, Karl. "The European Background of Contemporary Nihilism." In *Nature, History and Existentialism*. Ed. Arnold Levinson. Evanston, Ill.: Northwestern University Press, 1966.

Logstrup, K. E. "The Doctrines of God and Man in the Theology of Rudolf Bultmann." Trans. Johann Stochholm. In *The Theology of Rudolf Bultmann*. Ed. Charles W. Kegley. New York: Harper and Row, 1966, pp. 83–103.

Lundin, Robert. "Deconstructive Therapy." *The Reformed Journal* 36:1 (1986), pp. 15–20.

Lyotard, Jean-François. *The Postmodern Condition: A Report on Knowledge*. Trans. Geoff Bennington and Brian Massumi. Theory and History of Literature, vol. 10. Minneapolis: University of Minnesota, 1984.

McCarthy, Thomas. "Private Irony and Public Decency: Richard Rorty's New Pragmatism." *Critical Inquiry* 16 (1990), 355–71.

McConnachie, John. "The Teaching of Karl Barth: A New Positive Movement in German Theology." *Hibbert Journal* 25 (1927), 385–400.

McGrath, Alister. *The Making of Modern German Christolo-*

gy: From the Enlightenment to Pannenberg. New York: Basil Blackwell, 1986.

MacIntyre, Alisdair. *After Virtue: A Study in Moral Theory.* Notre Dame, Ind.: University of Notre Dame Press, 1984.

———. "Philosophy, the 'Other' Disciplines, and Their Histories: A Rejoinder to Richard Rorty." *Soundings* 65 (1982), 127–45.

Mackey, Louis. "Slouching Towards Bethlehem: Deconstructive Strategies in Theology." *Anglican Theological Review* 65 (1983), 255–72.

Mackintosh, Hugh Ross. *Types of Modern Theology: Schleiermacher to Barth.* London: Nisbet, 1947.

Macquarrie, John. "Existentialism." In *Encyclopedia of Religion.* Ed. Mircea Eliade et al. New York: Macmillan, 1986.

Magnus, Bernd. "Nietzsche and Postmodern Criticism." *Nietzsche Studien* 18 (1989), 301–16.

———. *Nietzsche's Existential Imperative.* Bloomington: Indiana University Press, 1978.

———. "Nietzsche's Philosophy in 1888: *The Will to Power* and the *Uebermensch.*" *Journal of the History of Philosophy* 24 (1986), 77–98.

Malantschuk, Gregor. *Kierkegaard's Thought.* Trans. Howard V. Hong and Edna H. Hong. Princeton: Princeton University Press, 1974.

Megill, Allan. *Prophets of Extremity: Nietzsche, Heidegger, Foucault, Derrida.* Berkeley and Los Angeles: University of California Press, 1985.

Miller, J. Hillis. "The Critic as Host." In *Deconstruction and Criticism.* New York: Seabury Press, 1979, pp. 216–253.

Moltmann, Juergen, ed. *Anfaenge der dialektischen Theologie.* 2 vols. Munich: Chr. Kaiser Verlag, 1962.

Mueller-Lauter, Wolfgang. "Der Idealismus als Nihilismus der Erkenntnis." *Theologia Viatorum: Jahrbuch der Kirchlichen Hochschule Berlin* 13 (1977), 133–53.

Nehamas, Alexander. *Nietzsche: Life as Literature.* Cambridge, Mass.: Harvard University Press, 1985.

Nicholls, William. *Systematic and Philosophical Theology.* The Pelican Guide to Modern Theology, vol. 1. Baltimore: Penguin Books, 1969.

Nicolai, Georg Friedrich. *Biologie des Krieges: Betrachtungen eines deutschen Naturforschers.* Zurich: Art Institut O. Fuessli, 1917. Trans. Constance A. Grande and Julian Grande, *The Biology of War.* New York: The Century Company, 1918.

Nietzsche, Friedrich. *The Antichrist.* In *The Portable Nietzsche.* Trans. and ed. Walter Kaufmann. New York: Penguin Books, 1982, pp.565–656.

———. *Daybreak.* Trans. R. J. Hollingdale. Cambridge, Mass.: Cambridge University Press, 1982.

———. *Ecce Homo: Or, How One Becomes What One Is.* In *Basic Writings of Nietzsche.* Trans. and ed. Walter Kaufmann. New York: Random House, 1968, pp. 657–800.

———. *The Gay Science.* Trans. Walter Kaufmann. New York: Vintage Books, 1974.

———. *Human, All-too-human.* Trans. Marion Faber. Lincoln: University of Nebraska Press, 1984.

———. *On the Genealogy of Morals.* In *Basic Writings of Nietzsche.* Trans. and ed. Walter Kaufmann. New York: The Modern Library, 1968, pp. 439–599.

———. *Saemtliche Werke: Kritische Studienausgabe in 15 Baenden.* Ed. Giorgio Colli and Mazzino Montinari. Munich: Deutscher Taschenbuch Verlag, 1980.

———. *Thus Spoke Zarathustra.* In *The Portable Nietzsche.* Trans. and ed. Walter Kaufmann. New York: Penguin, 1977, pp. 103–439.

———. *Twilight of the Idols.* In *The Portable Nietzsche.* Trans. and ed. Walter Kaufmann. New York: Penguin, 1977, pp. 463–564.

———. *The Will To Power.* Trans. Walter Kaufmann and R. J. Hollingdale. New York: Vintage Books, 1968.

Norris, Christopher. *The Contest of Faculties.* London: Methuen, 1981.

———. *The Deconstructive Turn: Essays in the Rhetoric of Philosophy.* New York: Methuen, 1984.

O'Leary, Joseph Stephen. *Questioning Back: The Overcoming of Metaphysics in Christian Tradition.* Minneapolis: Winston Press, 1985.

Overbeck, Franz. *Christentum und Kultur: Gedanken und Anmerkungen zur modernen Theologie.* Ed. Carl A. Bernouilli. Basel: Benno Schurabe, 1919.

Paterson, R. W. K. *The Nihilistic Egoist: Max Stirner.* London: Oxford University Press, 1971.

Paul, Jean [Johann Paul Friedrich Richter]. "Poetische Nihilisten." In *Vorschule der Aesthetik. Werke,* vol. V. Munich: Carl Hanser Verlag, 1963, pp. 459–60.

Poeggeler, Otto. "Hegel und die Anfaenge der Nihilismus-Diskussion." In *Der Nihilismus als Phaenomen der Geistesgeschichte in der wissenschaftlichen Diskussion unseres Jahrhundert.* Ed. Dieter Arendt. Darmstadt: Wissenschaftliche Buchgesellschaft, 1974.

Polanyi, Michael. *Beyond Nihilism.* Arthur Stanley Eddington Memorial Lecture 13. Cambridge: Cambridge University Press, 1960.

Popkin, Richard H. *The History of Skepticism.* Berkeley and Los Angeles: University of California Press, 1979.

Prado, C. G. *The Limits of Pragmatism.* Atlantic Highlands, N.J.: Humanities International Press, 1987.

Pribic, Rado. *Bonaventura's 'Nachtwachen' and Dostoyevsky's 'Notes from Underground': A Comparison in Nihilism.* Munich: Verlag Otto Sagner, 1974.

Rajchman, John and Cornel West, eds. *Post-Analytic Philosophy.* New York: Columbia University Press, 1985.

Romano, Carlin. "Naughty, Naughty: Richard Rorty Makes Philosophers Squirm." *Village Voice Literary Supplement* June 1987, pp. 14–18.

Rorty, Richard. *Consequences of Pragmatism (Essays: 1972–1980).* Minneapolis: University of Minnesota Press, 1982.

———. *Contingency, Irony, and Solidarity.* Cambridge: Cambridge University Press, 1989.

———. "Deconstruction and Circumvention." *Critical Inquiry* 11 (1984), pp. 1–23.

———. "From Logic to Language to Play: A Plenary Address to the InterAmerican Congress." *Proceedings*

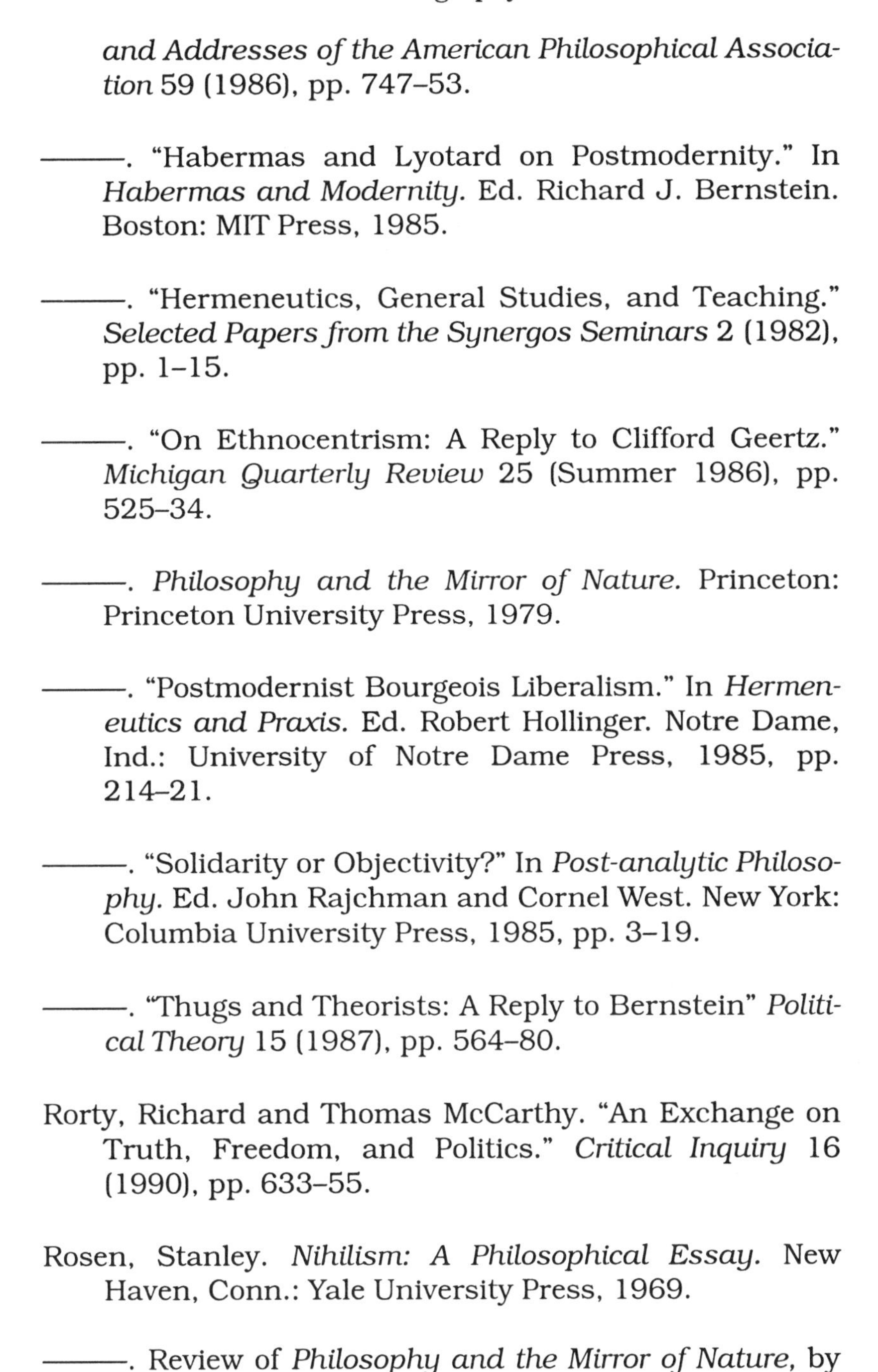

and Addresses of the American Philosophical Association 59 (1986), pp. 747–53.

———. "Habermas and Lyotard on Postmodernity." In *Habermas and Modernity*. Ed. Richard J. Bernstein. Boston: MIT Press, 1985.

———. "Hermeneutics, General Studies, and Teaching." *Selected Papers from the Synergos Seminars* 2 (1982), pp. 1–15.

———. "On Ethnocentrism: A Reply to Clifford Geertz." *Michigan Quarterly Review* 25 (Summer 1986), pp. 525–34.

———. *Philosophy and the Mirror of Nature*. Princeton: Princeton University Press, 1979.

———. "Postmodernist Bourgeois Liberalism." In *Hermeneutics and Praxis*. Ed. Robert Hollinger. Notre Dame, Ind.: University of Notre Dame Press, 1985, pp. 214–21.

———. "Solidarity or Objectivity?" In *Post-analytic Philosophy*. Ed. John Rajchman and Cornel West. New York: Columbia University Press, 1985, pp. 3–19.

———. "Thugs and Theorists: A Reply to Bernstein" *Political Theory* 15 (1987), pp. 564–80.

Rorty, Richard and Thomas McCarthy. "An Exchange on Truth, Freedom, and Politics." *Critical Inquiry* 16 (1990), pp. 633–55.

Rosen, Stanley. *Nihilism: A Philosophical Essay*. New Haven, Conn.: Yale University Press, 1969.

———. Review of *Philosophy and the Mirror of Nature*, by

Richard Rorty. *Review of Metaphysics* 33 (1980), pp. 799–802.

Rupp, George. *Culture-Protestantism: German Liberal Theology at the Turn of the Twentieth Century.* American Academy of Religion Studies in Religion Series, No. 15. Missoula, Mont: Scholars Press, 1977.

Santurri, Edward. Review of *The Flight from Authority,* by Jeffrey Stout. *Religious Studies Review* 9 (1983), pp. 330–4.

Sartre, Jean Paul. "Existentialism." Trans. Bernard Frechtman. In *Existentialism and Human Emotions.* New York: Philosophical Library, 1957, pp. 9–51.

Schacht, Richard. *Nietzsche.* London: Routledge and Kegan Paul, 1983.

———. "Nietzsche and Nihilism." In *Nietzsche: A Collection of Critical Essays.* Ed. Robert C. Solomon. Notre Dame, Ind.: University of Notre Dame Press, 1980, pp. 58–82.

Schempp, Paul. "Marginal Glosses on Barthianism." In *The Beginnings of Dialectical Theology,* vol. I. Trans. James M. Robinson. Richmond, Va.: John Knox Press, 1968.

Schleiermacher, Friedrich Ernst. *The Christian Faith.* 2 vols. Ed. H. R. Mackintosh and J. S. Stewart. New York: Harper and Row, 1965.

Seidel, George. *Being, Nothing, and God.* Assen: Van Gorcum and Co., 1970.

Shaw, Daniel. "Rorty and Nietzsche: Some Elective Affinities." *International Studies in Philosophy* 21:2 (Summer 1989), pp. 3–14.

Smart, James D. *The Divided Mind of Modern Theology:*

Karl Barth and Rudolf Bultmann, 1908–1933. Philadelphia: Westminster Press, 1967.

Solomon, Robert C. "Nietzsche, Nihilism, and Morality." In *Nietzsche: A Collection of Critical Essays.* Ed. Robert C. Solomon. Notre Dame, Ind.: University of Notre Dame Press, 1980, pp. 202–25.

Stepniak [Sergei Mikhailovich Kravchinskii]. *Underground Russia: Revolutionary Profiles and Sketches from Life.* Trans. from Italian. London: Smith, Elder, 1883.

Stirner, Max [Johann Kaspar Schmidt]. *The Ego and His Own.* Trans. Steven T. Byington. London: A. C. Fifield, 1913.

Stout, Jeffrey. *Ethics After Babel: The Languages of Morals and Their Discontents.* Boston: Beacon Press, 1988.

———. "A Lexicon of Post-modernism." *Religious Studies Review* 13 (1987), pp. 18–22.

———. "Liberal Society and the Languages of Morals." *Soundings* 69 (1986), pp. 32–59.

Taylor, Mark. "Descartes, Nietzsche and the Search for the Unsayable." *New York Times Book Review* Feb. 1, 1987, pp. 3–4.

———. *Erring: A Post-Modern A/Theology.* Chicago: University of Chicago Press, 1984.

Thielecke, Helmut. *Nihilism: Its Origin and Nature, with a Christian Answer.* Trans. John W. Doberstein. New York: Schocken Books, 1969.

Thurneysen, Eduard. *Dostoyevsky: A Theological Study.* Trans. Keith R. Crim. London: The Epworth Press, 1964.

Troeltsch, Ernst. *The Absoluteness of Christianity and the History of Religions*. Trans. David Reid. Richmond, Va.: John Knox Press, 1981.

Turgenev, Ivan. *Fathers and Sons*. Trans. Rosemary Edmonds. New York: Penguin, 1986.

Unger, Peter. "Skepticism and Nihilism." *Nous* 14 (1980), pp. 517–45.

Valadier, Paul. "Christliche Dekadenz und Wiederaufleben des Goettlichen: Die Ambivalenz Nietzsches und der Nietzsche-Interpretation." *Stimmen der Zeit* 196:6 (June 1978), pp. 395–406.

Vattimo, Gianni. *The End of Modernity: Nihilism and Hermeneutics in Postmodern Culture*. Trans. Jon R. Snyder. Baltimore: Johns Hopkins University Press, 1988.

Wingren, Gustav. *Theology in Conflict*. Trans. Eric H. Wahlstrom. Philadelphia: Muhlenberg Press, 1958.

Wood, David. "Derrida and the Paradoxes of Reflection." *Journal of the British Society for Phenomenology* 11:3 (1980), pp. 225–38.

Woodward, Kenneth. "A New Look at Lit Crit." *Newsweek*. June 22, 1981, 80–3.

Zahrnt, Hans. *The Question of God: Protestant Theology in the Twentieth Century*. Trans. R. A. Wilson. New York: Harcourt, Brace, and World, 1967.

Index